# *Your* COVENANT

# Your Covenant

MARK A. SHIELDS

CFI
An Imprint of Cedar Fort, Inc.
Springville, Utah

ISBN 13: 978-1-4621-1779-6

Published by CFI, an imprint of Cedar Fort, Inc.
2373 W. 700 S., Springville, UT 84663
Distributed by Cedar Fort, Inc., www.cedarfort.com

LIBRARY OF CONGRESS CATALOGING-IN-PUBLICATION DATA

Names: Shields, Mark A. (Mark Alan), author.
Title: Your covenant / Mark A. Shields.
Description: Springville, Utah : CFI, an imprint of Cedar Fort, Inc., [2016]
| "2016 | Includes bibliographical references.
Identifiers: LCCN 2015038460 | ISBN 9781462117796 (perfect bound : alk. paper)
Subjects: LCSH: Covenants--Religious aspects--Church of Jesus Christ of Latter-day Saints. | Covenants--Religious aspects--Mormon Church. | Temple endowments (Mormon Church) | Abraham (Biblical patriarch) | Church of Jesus Christ of Latter-day Saints--Doctrines. | Mormon Church--Doctrines.
Classification: LCC BX8657 .S55 2016 | DDC 231.7/6--dc23
LC record available at http://lccn.loc.gov/2015038460

Cover design by Shawnda T. Craig

Edited and typeset by Kevin Haws

Printed in Canada

10 9 8 7 6 5 4 3 2 1

Printed on acid-free paper

# Contents

# Section One

## Introduction to the Abrahamic Covenant

**When I was** a teenager, I was an aspiring world-class guitarist. That doesn't mean I was a world-class guitarist; it only means I wanted to be. Whenever I picked up a guitar and played what came naturally to me, I found myself trying to sound like my favorite jazz guitarist, George Benson. I loved his tone, fluidity, and astounding musicianship. Well, one night I had a dream. In that dream, I was granted a wish.

Naturally, I chose a wish that was in line with my adoration of George Benson. I asked to have the *talent* of George Benson. For some reason, I didn't ask to be able to play like George Benson; I only asked to have his *talent*—his ability. As soon as my wish was granted, I headed straight for my guitar and expected the notes to flow just as they would from my favorite virtuoso. It didn't happen. If anything, my playing had gone down a notch.

I woke up and immediately got the lesson: at least in my dream, I had talent on par with my hero all along; I just needed to develop it.

People tend to spend a lot of effort looking up to celebrities and other heroes. In looking to them as our role models, we may live our whole lives not fully realizing or appreciating the blessings we already have. And those blessings infinitely outshine the blessings we may envy in any other person. Many of us have been born into a promised blessing that offers eternal life in the presence of our Heavenly Father. Even more, this blessing offers us an eternal family greater than our minds can comprehend. And even *more* than that, the promised blessing also brings us the eternal rewards of the priesthood, to rule as kings or queens, beyond what we have heard in our favorite fairy tales. If we were not born into the promise of these blessings, we receive them when we are baptized, when the men among us receive the priesthood, and when we receive the blessings of the temple both in the endowment and in the sealing ordinances.

These are the blessings of the Abrahamic covenant. These blessings are not limited to our dreams, as it was with my favorite guitarist. In entering into the covenants of the holy temple, the promise of these is already upon us. We don't have to hope for a mythical genie or leprechaun to give us these blessings. We only have to keep the covenants we make in the holy temple.

Why do so few understand and appreciate these promises that are already ours? There are a handful of gospel topics that are commonly mentioned but not so commonly understood. Take, for example, the Atonement of Jesus Christ. Many scriptures and teachings leave no doubt that it is the most important act ever accomplished in earth's history and that we are all eternally cut off from the presence of God without it. That teaches us about its importance, and that is a lesson we as a church understand well.

But I spent many frustrating years trying to figure out exactly what act or acts actually constitute the Atonement. Was it in Gethsemane? Was it on Golgotha? Was it both? Or was it also in the Garden Tomb? Or was it even the Savior's entire life? After all, that entire life gave us a perfect example to follow in all things. Likewise, every minute of the Savior's life was necessary preparation for Him to pay the price of our sins, because every minute was lived without sin. With questions like these, I don't think I'm alone in my quest to understand to understand the Atonement better. I'm convinced that I would appreciate the Atonement more deeply and personally if I could define it and understand it better.

For that, I count the Atonement as an often discussed but somewhat superficially understood gospel topic. But it isn't the only important subject that is not well understood.

I'm sure that you can think of several other subjects in this same category.

Without a doubt, the Abrahamic covenant is the epitome of gospel subjects that Latter-day Saints simply don't understand or appreciate enough. We hear about it. We have a lesson about it every four years in Sunday school. We had perhaps one hour devoted to it in seminary. We are told that it is incredibly important (and it certainly is). Still, most of us have a shallow understanding of what it actually is, why it is so important, and how it relates to us.

This book was written specifically to answer those questions.

We will start with brief summaries to give you a working understanding of the covenant as you read the rest of the book. These summaries are provided to help you understand the rest of the book, not to give you a true understanding of the subject in just a few paragraphs.

## What Is the Abrahamic Covenant?

The Lord promised Abraham many general and specific blessings. He was promised that the Lord would prosper him in extraordinary ways. The greatest of these promises fall into three general categories:

- *Posterity.* Abraham was promised a family as numerous as the sand on the seashore and the stars in the heavens (Genesis 15:5; 22:17). He was also promised that this endless posterity would include kings (Genesis 17:6). This promise has been interpreted to mean that the Savior Jesus Christ would be born of Abraham's lineage.
- *Priesthood.* Abraham was blessed that he and his endless posterity would hold the priesthood and be the means of blessing every family on earth (Genesis 12:2–3).
- *Promised land (Genesis 17:8).* Abraham was promised the land of Canaan for himself and his endless posterity. This blessing must be understood symbolically to represent the celestial kingdom. Just as Canaan was the promised land where Moses

> led the children of Israel, the Abrahamic covenant leads us to the eternal promised land. Canaan is a scriptural representation of the celestial kingdom.

Thinking of the promised land as a representation of the celestial kingdom, it becomes clear that the blessings of the Abrahamic covenant—the blessings of eternal priesthood, eternal posterity, and the celestial kingdom—are the blessings of exaltation. The Lord gave Abraham this covenant as a way of blessing him in mortality and in eternity. The covenant was the Lord's way of promising and eventually sealing on Abraham the blessings of exaltation. It's the Lord's desire to bestow these same blessings on all of His children (Moses 1:39), and through this covenant, the Lord does just that for us.

Simply put, the blessings of the Abrahamic covenant are the blessings of exaltation and eternal life.

## What Does Abraham's Covenant Have to Do with Us?

In a word, everything. The most basic lesson to understand is that the Abrahamic covenant is not simply a piece of history. The Lord promised Abraham great blessings, but the covenant goes far beyond Abraham. The blessings promised to him are likewise promised to us through the ordinances and covenants of the gospel. In the latter-days, the Lord has taught us, "This promise is yours also, because ye are of Abraham" (D&C 132:31).

The covenant is named after Abraham because Abraham's account of the blessings and requirements of the covenant is the most complete we have in the scriptures. But the mere naming of the covenant does not restrict it to Abraham any more than naming the Melchizedek Priesthood after Melchizedek restricts that priesthood to him. The covenant is named after Abraham, but it is eternal and based on eternal gospel laws. That means the covenant applies to every son of Adam and daughter of Eve. Make no mistake about it—this covenant is intended for us.

## How Do We Enter into This Covenant?

As with any essential covenant, we enter into the Abrahamic covenant by receiving ordinances. The Bible Dictionary teaches that Abraham received the first ordinances of baptism and confirmation, which the Bible Dictionary calls "the covenant of salvation" (see the Bible Dictionary, "Abraham, covenant of"). These are the first ordinances that unlock the blessings of the Abrahamic covenant.

But the Abrahamic covenant isn't just about salvation; it is about exaltation—living the kind of life that Heavenly Father lives and inheriting all that the "Father hath" (D&C 84:38). On this subject, the Bible Dictionary states that Abraham received the higher ordinances of the temple, which the aforementioned Bible Dictionary section calls "the covenant of exaltation."

These higher ordinances of the temple comprise the true substance of the Abrahamic covenant—"the covenant of exaltation." On this topic, Elder John A. Widtsoe succinctly taught, "Temple worship is an avenue to exaltation in God's kingdom."[1] Hugh Nibley added, "Doing the works of Abraham centers around the temple."[2]

The first ordinances of the gospel provide the keys to salvation and membership in God's kingdom on earth, namely His Church.

The higher ordinances—the ordinances of the temple—pertain to exaltation and eternal life, the greatest of God's gifts. This is the true import of the Abrahamic covenant. Therefore, the most complete answer to the question is that we enter into the Abrahamic covenant's full blessings through the ordinances of the temple. The Abrahamic covenant is all about the temple.

I will candidly share that when I first received my endowment, the only gospel teaching that was readily apparent to me in the endowment ceremony was the Abrahamic covenant. As we will see, references to that covenant are woven throughout the temple experience. They are everywhere. On that note, think of this book as a guide to recognizing the Abrahamic covenant in the temple. As you read, think of the temple ordinances that point particularly to each of the promised blessings of the Abrahamic covenant. Reflect on the ordinances that lead to eternal priesthood offices. Then think on the ordinances that point directly toward the promised celestial kingdom. Finally, recognize the ordinances that lead to eternal posterity. All three of these blessings are unmistakably prefigured in the ordinances of the temple.

To teach of the Abrahamic covenant without teaching of the temple—or teaching the temple without understanding the Abrahamic covenant—is like trying to explain the ocean without mentioning water. The two are inseparable. The covenant is only accessed through the ordinances of the temple, and it is not an oversimplification to say that the temple's main purpose is to bestow the blessings of the Abrahamic covenant.

## What Do We Need to Do to Receive These Blessings?

"Go ye, therefore, and do the works of Abraham" (D&C 132:32). Covenants require action on our part. It isn't enough just to make a covenant and expect the blessings to flow from it. We have to keep the covenant to receive the blessings associated with it. "There is a law, irrevocably decreed in heaven before the foundations of this world, upon which all blessings are predicated—and when we obtain any blessing from God, it is by obedience to that law upon which it is predicated" (D&C 130:20–21).

The words *commandment*, *law*, and *covenant* may be used somewhat interchangeably because of this great truth taught in the Doctrine and Covenants. Covenants are the Lord's way of bestowing blessings, and obedience to those covenants constitutes obedience to the commandments—the laws of God. Keeping covenants consists of obeying the laws that comprise the covenant. In other words, keep the covenant (obey the law), and you receive the blessings. The formula is so simple that we can lose sight of it or doubt it.

The "works of Abraham" mentioned previously are perhaps the part of the covenant that we understand the least. Many biblical scholars have concluded that the Abrahamic covenant was simply a blessing the Lord gave Abraham. Well, it is not a covenant unless there is some action required. Anciently, those requirements were specific to Abraham. In our day, we have access to the same blessings by following the same example shown by Abraham.

The Abrahamic covenant is unique because both the blessings and the works (the laws or commandments) are revealed over the course of several chapters in the Bible and the Pearl of Great Price. In the Bible, it runs from Genesis 12 to 22. In the Pearl of Great Price, Abraham 1 gives extremely valuable background information about the covenant, which is then revealed in chapter 2. The principle blessings of the covenant are promised multiple times over the course of these chapters and the decades that they cover. In several of those chapters, the Lord gives Abraham specific instructions—commandments or laws—that immediately precede the promise of the blessings. These commandments are the works of Abraham that we need to do to receive the blessings promised. Whether the specific commandments given to Abraham are literal or symbolic is not the point; the true message is that each of the laws given to Abraham teaches a gospel principle and commandment to us.

Earlier, I stated that this subject is perhaps what we understand the least about the Abrahamic covenant. This is what I mean—most biblical commentaries and manuals (even in the Church) list or focus on only one chapter of Genesis in examining the Abrahamic covenant. Even the Abrahamic covenant entry on the Church website cites only Genesis 17 and Abraham 2–3. Other commentaries only cite Genesis 12 or 15. That doesn't give the full picture, especially of "the works of Abraham" that unlock the blessings of the covenant.

Briefly summarized, these acts include:

- *A great demonstration of obedience and faith (Genesis 12).* The Lord commanded Abraham to leave his home and follow the Lord to a land that He would reveal. This is known in biblical circles as "the call." It accompanies the first great and complete promise of blessings to Abraham.
- *The offering of sacrifices (Genesis 15).* The second time the Lord iterated the promises of the covenant to Abraham, He commanded him to offer specific sacrifices. The law of sacrifices accompanies and parallels the principle of repentance.
- *"Walk before me, and be thou perfect" (Genesis 17:1).* This is a commandment to live by every principle of the gospel. This

commandment was given on the third complete promise of the covenant blessings to Abraham. As walking symbolically represents the way we live, this commandment parallels the ordinance of baptism—it represents a new life, walking before God in obedience to all His commandments. In the same chapter, the Lord also gave unto Abraham the commandment of circumcision as "a token of the covenant" (Genesis 17:11).

- *The sacrifice of all things (Genesis 22).* Abraham was commanded to offer the thing he valued most in all of life: his beloved son Isaac.

Through all of the translations and the history of the Bible, the Lord maintained the full account of Abraham receiving the covenant on multiple occasions in Genesis. Each time He gave the promises of the covenant to Abraham, different nuances were revealed and different laws were given. If we think of the Abrahamic covenant as a ladder reaching to heaven (and we see exactly this in Genesis 28), we cannot afford to skip any rungs on that ladder, figuratively speaking, as that would make for a treacherous and potentially disastrous climb. This book looks at each of the principal rungs of the Abrahamic covenant in much more detail than the brief summary given previously. In doing so, we will learn much more fully of the works of Abraham that lead to the blessings of Abraham.

## Adding Abraham and Sarah to Adam and Eve as Our Examples

The temple and the Creation accounts in the scriptures teach us from the perspective of Adam and Eve. They are our role models in our own journey from the tree of knowledge of good and evil back to the tree of life and the eternal presence of God. Their very names are lessons and references to us. Adam means "mankind" in biblical Hebrew and Eve is the feminine adjective for "living." The name Adam is therefore a reference to all of us, while Eve is a reference to the life that can only come through a mother. Adam and Eve's journey—from the presence of God in premortal life through the Fall and mortality, and back to the tree of life and the eternal presence of God—is our journey.

As we are instructed to do the "works of Abraham," we have another most precious and instructive set of role models: Abraham and Sarah. The covenant that bestows the blessings of exaltation is named after Abraham, and there are no such blessings without Sarah, so it only makes sense that the Lord teaches indispensable lessons of the path to eternal life through Abraham and Sarah. The scriptures give magnificent details on covenants and trials through Abraham and Sarah that we simply don't have in the accounts of Adam and Eve. Seeing Abraham and Sarah as role models for our own path to the blessings of eternal life is essential and enlightening.

So just as Adam and Eve's journey back to the presence of God is our journey, Abraham's covenant is our covenant. The blessings promised to Abraham are the blessings of returning to the presence of God, and they are ours. The works that Abraham and Sarah were commanded to do help mark the same path back to the presence of God that we must follow.

The word *covenant* comes from two Latin roots: *con*, meaning "together" or "with," and *venire*, meaning "to come." Therefore, a covenant is literally a "coming together" of two people. The Lord is known as the God of Abraham, Isaac, and Jacob because of the Abrahamic covenant. He is our God, and we are His people because we have the blessing of coming together with Him through this covenant. We have access to the same blessings promised to Abraham if we will do "the works of Abraham," following the example of Abraham and Sarah.

## Recognizing the Covenant in the Scriptures

Earlier, I made a somewhat bold statement about the importance of the Abrahamic covenant and our need to learn more about it. Though you may be raising your eyebrows at this, it's true. In fact, the scriptures are absolutely replete with references to the Abrahamic covenant. Obviously, one would expect Jesus Christ to be the most common theme in the scriptures, whether He is explicitly named or implicitly referenced. He is certainly the central figure of the gospel and the scriptures and may rightfully be called the only true hero in the scriptures because He is involved every scriptural success story.

Still, the relative rarity of the Savior's name in the scriptures may be a little surprising. Online research reveals that the Savior is never mentioned by His earthly name in the Old Testament. Through all the prophecies of His coming, only Book of Mormon prophets state His actual name, Jesus, in their prophecies. Likewise, one of His titles, *Redeemer*, appears eighty-two times in the scriptures but is somehow completely absent from the New Testament. Two more of His titles, *the Holy One of Israel* and *Messiah*, are found seventy-eight and fifty-six times respectively but are likewise nowhere in the New Testament. Perhaps most surprising, the sum and substance of His ministry—the Atonement—appears as a word only once in the New Testament, even though it is found ninety-nine times in the rest of the standard works.

Despite the conspicuous absence of some of His titles, I have no doubt the Lord would be the most common and prevalent theme and figure in the scriptures if I had the mental or spiritual patience or the time to plug all of His names, titles, and other references to Him into the search engine.

But the Abrahamic covenant isn't far behind in its saturation of the scriptures. The name Israel, the name of the Lord's covenant people, is an Abrahamic covenant reference. It is the covenant that led to Israel's birth and chosen status as the Lord's covenant people. Israel was the new name given to the patriarch Jacob following a sacred experience recorded in Genesis 32:28. According to the Bible Dictionary, a reference to Israel is a reference not just to one man but also to the entire nation or nations of his descendants, as well as the Lord's covenant people. That covenant and bloodline did not begin with Jacob or even with his father, Isaac. It was only passed through them. The covenant and, therefore, the name *Israel* actually began two generations before Jacob with the great patriarch Abraham and his covenant with the Lord. References to the "God of Israel" or the "God of Abraham, Isaac, and Jacob" indicate the familial bond that comes through the covenant established with the great patriarch Abraham.

Other "gods" abounded in the Old Testament, but the God of Abraham, Isaac, and Jacob or the God of Israel is unique for obvious reasons. Besides being the only true and living God, the Father of all, the Creator of worlds without end, the Author of the plan of salvation, He was also a personal God to Israel. This God had made personal and sure promises to them (and to us). This God was their God because of the covenant, specifically the Abrahamic covenant.

References to Israel appear 2,528 times in the scriptures. Each of them is a real reference to the Abrahamic covenant, just as any mention to the Atonement, Redeemer, Savior, or countless other words and titles is a reference to Jesus Christ.

The references don't stop there either. As we will see, the temple goes hand in hand with the Abrahamic covenant. The temple is there for many purposes and functions (see Doctrine and Covenants 124:39), but by and large the main functions of the temple are the ordinances of the Abrahamic covenant. In this respect, scriptural references to the temple are often references to the Abrahamic covenant as well. As you search the scriptures, you may come to recognize many, many more references throughout the inspired writings.

Together, these terms relating to the Abrahamic covenant appear well over three thousand times in the scriptures. And, unlike several other names and titles associated with the main subject of the scriptures—the Savior—these references are prevalent throughout all four standard works.

By contrast, references to repentance appear 951 times in the scriptures. Faith appears 861 times. Love is mentioned about 550 times. Mercy appears 520 times.

These are all extremely important gospel subjects, but they are not nearly as prevalent as the Abrahamic covenant. In fact, there is only one scripture that the Lord thought important enough to include in all four standard works: the prophecy of Elijah's return. This ultra-important scripture is also a reference to the Abrahamic covenant.

The first reference is in Malachi 4, the closing chapter of the Old Testament: "For, behold, the day cometh, that shall burn as an oven; and all the proud, yea, and all that do wickedly, shall be stubble: and the day that cometh shall burn them up, saith the Lord of hosts, that it shall leave them neither root nor branch. . . . Behold, I will send you Elijah the prophet before the coming of the great and dreadful day of the Lord: and he shall turn the heart of the fathers to the children, and the heart of the children to their fathers, lest I come and smite the earth with a curse" (Malachi 4:1, 5–6).

When the Savior appeared the Nephites following His Resurrection, He taught them the same lesson and repeated the same scripture to them (3 Nephi 25).

In the Pearl of Great Price, Joseph Smith recounted this same scripture, as the angel Moroni taught it to him. This time, the scripture was given somewhat different.

> For behold, the day cometh that shall burn as an oven, and all the proud, yea, and all that do wickedly shall burn as stubble; for they that come shall burn them, saith the Lord of Hosts, that it shall leave them neither root nor branch. . . . Behold, I will reveal unto you the Priesthood, by the hand of Elijah the prophet, before the coming of the great and dreadful day of the Lord. . . . And he shall plant in the hearts of the children the promises made to the fathers, and the hearts of the children shall turn to their fathers. If it were not so, the whole earth would be utterly wasted at his coming. (Joseph Smith History 1:37–39)

Finally, Doctrine and Covenants 2:1–3 teaches:

> Behold, I will reveal unto you the Priesthood, by the hand of Elijah the prophet, before the coming of the great and dreadful day of the Lord. And he shall plant in the hearts of the children the promises made to the fathers, and the hearts of the children shall turn to their fathers. If it were not so, the whole earth would be utterly wasted at his coming.

The same passage is repeated, in large part, in Doctrine and Covenants 27:9 and 110:13–16.

In four different works of scripture, we're specifically taught of Elijah's prophesied return and mission to plant the "promises made to the fathers" in the hearts of the children. These promises are so central, important, and transcendent that the Lord had them included in every book of latter-day scripture. When this prophecy was fulfilled, as recorded in Doctrine and Covenants 110, the gospel was fully restored.

So what are these "promises made to the fathers" to be restored in the last days by the hand of Elijah? They are none other than the promises made to Abraham, Isaac, and Jacob—the promises of receiving the gospel, the priesthood, eternal life, and a land of inheritance.[3] They are the blessings of the Abrahamic covenant.

In this sense, the scriptures are essentially teaching us that the Lord will restore the Abrahamic covenant through the prophet Elijah to usher in the last dispensation. The dispensation of the fulness of times was not fully underway until this prophecy was fulfilled on April 3, 1836 (see Doctrine and Covenants 110). In other words, the gospel of Jesus Christ had not been restored in all its fulness and glory until the keys to the blessings of Abraham, Isaac, and Jacob were restored.

As we learn to recognize and understand the references to Israel, the God of Abraham, Isaac, and Jacob, and the many other references to the Abrahamic covenant, we will find that these references appear in more chapters and on more pages of the scriptures than not.

You may find yourself—like me—whispering, "That's an Abrahamic covenant reference" throughout your scripture study and even while singing some hymns. You will then begin to recognize the scale and near omnipresence of the covenant the Lord has reserved for you in the latter days. You will start seeing yourself as a son or daughter of Abraham.

The conclusion is inescapable. The Abrahamic covenant ranks right up there with the Savior Himself as the most prominent theme in the scriptures. Yes, this is a subject we need to learn more about and appreciate to a greater extent.

## A Note on the Temple

It was stated earlier that the Abrahamic covenant and the temple are inseparable. This is not just a book about covenants; in fact, the central messages here all focus on the temple.

I am the first to acknowledge that the higher ordinances of the gospel found in the temple tend to be a bit overwhelming. If you're one of those people praying for a better understanding of the temple, let me assure you that you are not alone. Don't panic. The temple was designed in such a way that we never stop learning from it as long as we truly seek to do so.

The Savior Himself taught a lesson that should comfort all of us in our lack of understanding. John 13 tells the story of the Savior washing the feet of His disciples: "He riseth from supper, and laid aside his garments; and took a towel, and girded himself. After that he poureth water into a basin, and began to wash the disciples' feet, and to wipe them with the towel wherewith he was girded. Then cometh he to Simon Peter: and Peter saith unto him, Lord, dost thou wash my feet? Jesus answered and said unto him, What I do thou knowest not now; but thou shalt know hereafter" (John 13:4–7).

With insight from Doctrine and Covenants 88—the revelation known as the "olive leaf" plucked from paradise—we learn that the Savior was not just performing a customary act of service; He was performing a most sacred ordinance, one that brings deeply holy blessings (D&C 88:139). This was used to receive select people into the School of the Prophets and to pronounce them "clean from the blood of this generation" (D&C 88:138), just as the Savior administered it to pronounce His disciples "clean every whit" (John 13:10).

The *blessing* that accompanied this ordinance—of being pronounced clean—seems simple enough to understand. However, the *ordinance* that leads to this blessing is not so simple. The chief Apostle Peter—as devoted, blessed, and chosen as he was—displayed little understanding of the magnitude of this ordinance. Remember the Savior's words to him: "What I do thou knowest not now; but thou shalt know hereafter" (John 13:7). The Savior meant no shame in telling Peter this. It was simply the nature of the situation. A finite mortal mind doesn't easily digest an infinite spiritual lesson.

So it is with us. We receive ordinances in the gospel of Jesus Christ that we simply do not understand. This is particularly true of the ordinances, covenants, and blessings of the Abrahamic covenant administered in the temple. We may not know now, but with faith, prayer, righteous living, and repetition, we come to understand them in due time, long after we first receive them. How interesting it is that we grow line upon line, precept upon precept, grace for grace, all to understand blessings promised to us and ordinances received years and decades before.

Like Peter, we will be slow to gain an understanding of the ordinances and covenants that point us toward such blessings and unlock the gates leading to them. Just as Peter needed multiple teaching moments from the Savior before he fully embraced the ordinance, we need to return to the temple often to open our eyes and minds to the deeper meaning being conveyed by the ordinances.

That is how the Lord has designed it. The process of understanding the higher ordinances of the gospel takes time, among many other things, and it is a most exquisitely beautiful and rewarding process.

Latter-day prophets and Apostles have spoken plainly on our lack of understanding of the ordinances and blessings of the holy temple. In 1835, more than six years before the full endowment was restored in Nauvoo, Joseph Smith taught, "The endowment you are so anxious about, you cannot comprehend now, nor could Gabriel explain it to the understanding of your dark minds; but strive to be prepared in your hearts, be faithful in all things, that when we meet in the solemn assembly, that is, when such as God shall name out of all the official members shall meet, we must be clean every whit."[4] Joseph was not even speaking of the full endowment that we now have.[5] Even so, he openly taught that the limited ordinances revealed to that point were beyond the comprehension of the Saints at the time.

Are we any different in our understanding of the temple? Do we understand the scope of the blessings of the Atonement pronounced in the temple? Do we really absorb the lessons in the temple ordinances that reveal and unlock those blessings?

Elder Boyd K. Packer related a story of the great prophet David O. McKay, who also acknowledged having a less-than-perfect understanding of the ordinances of the temple.

> Not long before he died, when on infrequent occasions he would come to our meetings, he stood one day in the meeting and began to discuss the temple ceremony, the endowment. I will never forget! He stood there in that tall majesty that was typical of him. He had his big, bony hands on his chest and looked at the ceiling as he began to quote the endowment. (We were assembled there in the upper room [of the temple] and it was not inappropriate to discuss that there.) He quoted it at some great length. We were enthralled and inspired and knew we were witnessing a great moment. Then he stopped and looked again at the ceiling for a moment or two. Then he said, "I think I'm finally beginning to understand." That was very comforting to me. After nearly sixty-four years as an Apostle, he still had

> things that he was learning. Then we knew we were in the presence of not only the teacher who was teaching, but of a student who was learning.[6]

What a great story! Here are two of the greatest doctrinal minds and spiritual leaders who ever walked the earth. President McKay had served as a special witness of the name of Jesus Christ for nearly sixty-four years when he proclaimed that he was "finally beginning to understand" the endowment. Elder Packer, also a special witness of the Savior, took comfort in knowing there was still much to learn about the endowment, even for a man as great and tenured as President McKay.

Again, how different are we in our understanding of the sacred ordinances and blessings of the temple?

Like President McKay and Elder Packer, we shouldn't be ashamed of lack of understanding, nor should we stop trying to gain understanding. On the subject of temple preparation, Elder John A. Widtsoe taught in 1921,

> Colonel Willard Young said last night, in casual conversation, that we should give more attention to preparing our young people and some of the older people, for the work they are to do in the temple. He is undoubtedly right in his view. It is not quite fair to let the young girl or young man enter the temple unprepared, unwarned, if you choose, with no explanation of the glorious possibilities of the first fine day in the temple. Neither is it quite fair to pass opinion on temple worship after one day's participation followed by an absence of many years. The work should be repeated several times in quick succession, so that the lessons of the temple may be fastened upon the mind.[7]

Despite our limited understanding of these ordinances, we press forward and continue to attend the temple because we have faith in Christ. As the Prophet Joseph admonished, we strive to be faithful in all things—to be prepared in our hearts—that we may grow in understanding and one day be found clean every whit. We trust that the assurance the Savior gave to Peter of understanding these things in due time is an assurance for us as well.

## A Note on Sacredness

There is no other way to say it—this subject is extremely sacred. Because, as many prophets have taught, the higher blessings of this covenant and the priesthood order that administers the covenant are only received in the house of the Lord, they must be spoken of with the greatest of reverence. This topic is deserving of the most reverent treatment we can give it.

Because this subject, like any temple subject, is so sacred, many people simply remain silent on it, choosing not to study or discuss it for fear of saying something inappropriate. The Lord clearly expects us to treat sacred things in sacred ways, but I don't think He wants us to remain in silence either. Many of the points on this subject come from an address by President Ezra Taft Benson called, "What I hope you will teach your children about the temple."[8] The title of this discourse is a direct invitation from a latter-day prophet of God both to learn and to teach our children about this topic. At the invitation of a prophet, we certainly should be discussing this! Our challenge is to do so within the bounds of sacredness that the temple deserves.

To protect the sanctity of this subject, this book will only quote the scriptures or the teachings of the Brethren. If a truth is only taught in the temple, it will remain only in the temple. On the other hand, if the scriptures or the General Authorities of the Church have taught a temple truth publicly, that teaching is for our edification. Not only *can* we speak of such doctrine outside the temple, we *should* speak of it. You will clearly recognize many of the quotes and scriptures in this book as temple teachings, but you will need to connect the dots on your own with the guidance of the Holy Ghost—and based on the teachings that are only received in the temple.

As you follow President Ezra Taft Benson's invitation to discuss these teachings with your children and others, I invite you to pause at points and listen for the promptings of the Holy Ghost before you speak. If you feel the Spirit withdraw in any way, consider that an invitation from the Spirit to rethink either the content or the environment of your discussion. Sacred things must be kept in their sacred places. This book isn't written to appear sensational, and it is certainly not written to be controversial. The sole point of this book is to teach and edify by giving a deeper understanding of the Abrahamic covenant and the temple, where the covenant is administered in its fulness.

## The Exploration Guide

If we are heirs to the Abrahamic covenant—and we are—then we need to unwrap every last present under the Christmas tree, figuratively speaking. If that isn't possible because there are so many, we at least should to unwrap as many as we possibly can.

Here is the outline to help us unwrap those proverbial presents:

- This book is divided into three sections. The first section gives background information that will be a helpful foundation for the principles in the rest of the book. The foundation includes this introduction, a quick reference chart of the scriptures where the Abrahamic covenant is given, and a summary chapter on biblical covenants in general.
- The second section details the blessings of the covenant as revealed in Genesis and the Pearl of Great Price, including the patriarchal order of the priesthood that prefaces the covenant in the Pearl of Great Price. This is the Lord's part of the covenant.
- The third section details what was required of Abraham in those same chapters. This is our part of the covenant and what we need to do to receive these blessings. These are "the works of Abraham" that we are commanded to do to receive the blessings of Abraham (D&C 132:32).

Each chapter in these sections also relates the lessons to the temple, where the covenant is administered. In order to be cautious and reverent when teaching of the temple, you, the reader, will have to connect many of the dots that are temple references on your own, using your spiritual eyes and spiritual ears to recognize and apply these sacred lessons, just as the Savior asked His disciples to do when learning from His parables (Matthew 13:9–17). To those who do so, the Savior promised "more abundance" (Matthew 13:12). That promise of "more abundance" rings especially true when it comes to a discussion of the temple and its blessings.

This is a marvelous, glorious, and most sacred subject. Enjoy.

Each chapter in this book closes with summary bullet points for reference and review.

- *The Abrahamic covenant is for us today. It was renewed through Abraham's descendants, including modern Israel, or the members of The Church of Jesus Christ of Latter-day Saints.*
- *The principal blessings of the Abrahamic covenant are those of eternal posterity, eternal priesthood, and the celestial kingdom, symbolized by the promised land of Canaan.*
- *We enter into this covenant and gain access to these same blessings through the ordinances of the gospel. The ordinances of the temple are the principal ordinances of the Abrahamic covenant.*
- *Broadly speaking, the ordinances of the temple, in their respective groups, lead and point to each of these three great blessings of the Abrahamic covenant. To receive these blessings, we must do "the works of Abraham," meaning we must keep the covenants we make.*
- *The familiar prophecy of Elijah returning to the earth to plant the blessings made to the fathers in the hearts of the children is the only scripture found in all four standard works. It too is a reference to the Abrahamic covenant.*
- *Our dispensation of the fulness of times was not officially opened—and the Restoration was not complete—until this covenant and sealing power were restored.*
- *The covenant is administered today through the ordinances of the temple.*
- *Though we will not immediately understand all the temple covenants, making the connection between the Abrahamic covenant and the ordinances of the temple should help many people grow in their understanding of the holy temple.*
- *We are invited both to learn and to teach this subject, but we must take care to preserve its sanctity. We can do so by restricting our comments and quotes to the scriptures and the teachings of the General Authorities of the Church and by following the promptings of the Holy Ghost.*

# A Summary Chart of the Abrahamic Covenant

***The account of*** the Abrahamic covenant in the Old Testament goes from Genesis 12 to 22. The backdrop of Genesis 12 is, interestingly, the story of the Tower of Babel and Abraham's fathers through Shem. Abraham 1 gives more light on this story and tells us that Abraham's family, though descendants of kings and bearers of the priesthood, had fallen into apostasy. Abraham then was spared from the idolatrous altar of sacrifice and traveled from Ur to Haran and finally to Canaan.

Against this backdrop, Abraham 1 gives the account of Abraham seeking "greater happiness and peace and rest" through "the blessings of the fathers, and the right whereunto I should be ordained to administer the same" (Abraham 1:2). In Abraham 2 and its somewhat parallel account in Genesis 12,[9] Abraham found those "blessings of the fathers" and the "greater happiness and peace and rest" that this great "follower of righteousness" sought (Abraham 1:2).

In chart form, the Lord reveals the Abrahamic covenant as follows:

| Scripture | God Promises | God Commands |
|---|---|---|
| Genesis 12:1; Abraham 2:3 | | "Get thee out . . . unto a land I will shew thee" |
| Genesis 12:2–3 | Will be made a great nation<br>The Lord will bless Abraham<br>Abraham's name will be great<br>A great blessing to the families of the earth<br>Will bless them that bless Abraham (see Abraham 2:9–11)<br>Will curse them that curse Abraham (see Abraham 2:9–11) | |
| Genesis 12:7 | Canaan (see also Genesis 13:15; 15:9–11, 17; and Abraham 2:13–20) | |
| Genesis 13:14 | | Lift up thine eyes |
| Genesis 13:15 | Canaan | |
| Genesis 13:16 | Seed as the dust of the earth | |
| Genesis 13:17 | | Arise and walk through the land |
| Genesis 15:5 | Posterity like the stars | Look now toward heaven |
| Genesis 15:9–10 | | Sacrifices offered to memorialize the covenant |
| Genesis 15:13 | | Trials and captivity prophesied |

| | | |
|---|---|---|
| Genesis 17:1 | | Walk before God and be perfect |
| Genesis 17:4 | Father of many nations | |
| Genesis 17:5 | Abraham (Abram's) name changed for being a father of many nations | |
| Genesis 17:6 | Kings will come from Abraham—the Savior born through his lineage | |
| Genesis 17:7–8 | The Lord will be a God to Abraham and his seed | |
| Genesis 17:10–11 | | Circumcision given as token of the covenant |
| Genesis 17:15 | Sarah (Sarai's) name changed as part of her role in the covenant | |
| Genesis 17:20–21 | Ishmael will become a great nation, but the covenant will be carried through Isaac | |
| Genesis 18:10 | Sarah promised that she would have Isaac | |
| Genesis 21:2 | Sarah gave birth to Isaac in the covenant | |
| Genesis 22:2 | | Sacrifice his beloved son Isaac |

| | | |
|---|---|---|
| Genesis 22:17 | Stars and sand | |
| Genesis 22:17 | Victory over enemies | |
| Genesis 22:18 | All nations of the earth blessed in his seed | |
| Genesis 24:60 | Covenant renewed through Rebekah in a blessing | |
| Genesis 26:1–4 | Covenant renewed through Isaac | |
| Genesis 26:24–25 | Covenant again renewed through Isaac | |
| Genesis 27:28–29 | Covenant renewed through Jacob in a patriarchal blessing | |
| Genesis 28:1–4 | Covenant renewed through Jacob in a patriarchal blessing | |
| Genesis 28:10–15 | Covenant renewed through Jacob | |
| Genesis 35:10–12 | Covenant renewed through Jacob | |
| Genesis 48:3–4 | Covenant renewed through Jacob's grandsons, Ephraim and Manasseh | |

Comparing the Abrahamic covenant to a building, this chart is the frame of the covenant. The foundation of the covenant is the Atonement. The land on which the covenant is built is the temple—and its local counterpart, the home.

With that in mind, we will now construct the rest of the building that is the Abrahamic covenant, so to speak. A closer examination of the scriptures will help reveal the plumbing, the drywall, the electrical, the heating and cooling, and everything else in this magnificent structure.

# Biblical Covenants and Their Essential Components

A **deeper understanding** of biblical covenants and their composition sheds a great deal of light on the Abrahamic covenant. This chapter is a primer on biblical covenants. The principle of covenants is eternal. God the Father has always desired to bless His children, and He has always done so through covenants. From before the Creation, the pattern remains the same—we keep a commandment and live a law and receive the promised blessing attached to that commandment and law (D&C 130:19–20). That is how a covenant works. Beautifully simple, isn't it?

The Lord instructed us, "Draw near unto me and I will draw near unto you; seek me diligently and ye shall find me; ask, and ye shall receive; knock, and it shall be opened unto you" (D&C 88:63). Covenants work as we do our part, for the Lord most assuredly does His. Our part is keeping the commandments, drawing near unto the Lord, asking the Lord, and knocking at the Lord's door; His part is drawing near unto us, bestowing gifts on us, and opening doors for us. As we do our part, we can be assured that the Lord will do His. In fact, many times the Lord opens doors before we knock and gives us gifts before we ask for them or merit them in any way. This pattern is eternal, even from before the Creation.

The scriptures, particularly the book of Abraham, plainly teach that those who accepted Heavenly Father's plan in the premortal existence were blessed to come to earth, receive physical bodies, and be tried and rewarded with the blessings of earth life. These children are described as having kept "their first estate" (Abraham 3:26, 28; Jude 1:6). Likewise, those who keep their second estate will receive an eternal glory (Abraham 3:26). This keeping of estates suggests a reference to covenants and keeping them. In the case of our first estate, these scriptures suggest that we, as children of Heavenly Father, are here on earth because of premortal covenants. We have received the blessings of earth, of life because of our first estate covenants. Our lives come through covenants!

## The Edenic Covenant

The Lord has followed this pattern of covenants to bless His children throughout the dispensations of the earth, beginning with the Creation. When Adam was placed in the Garden of Eden, he was given beautiful and choice blessings. Adam was blessed with the Garden of Eden, a land divinely prepared and granted to him (Genesis 2:8). He was given dominion over all things in that land and even the whole earth (Genesis 1:28). He was given free access to every tree in the garden, with one exception (Genesis 2:16–17). Among the fruit available to Adam was the fruit of the tree of life, which we are later taught represents the love of God and even eternal life and the presence of God (1 Nephi 11:25; Revelation 22:14). Perhaps the greatest blessing given to Adam was his eternal companion, Eve (Genesis 2:18; 21–25).

To obtain and enjoy these blessings, Adam and Eve had to obey God's commandments. Those commandments specifically included taking care of the garden they were given (Genesis 2:15), not eating of the tree of knowledge of good and evil (Genesis 2:17), and (the first commandment given on earth) to multiply and replenish (meaning fill) the earth (Genesis 1:28).

Here, we see the pattern covenant was given to Adam and Eve. While the scriptures teach little about our first estate, they record Adam and Eve's experience in the Garden of Eden. Our Father in Heaven wanted to bless them, so He provided commandments as the way to receive those blessings. Because the Lord gave Adam and Eve specific commandments and blessings, the first chapters of Genesis set forth what may properly be called the Edenic covenant.

## Other Biblical Covenants

Adam and Eve partook of the fruit of tree of knowledge of good and evil, transgressing one of the commandments given to them. Because of this, they were cast out of the Garden of Eden and lost some of these promised blessings. Specifically, they lost the land prepared especially for them. They likewise lost their free access to the tree of life. No, they were not commanded to abstain from eating from the tree of life. Instead, they were protected from eating from it because they were not worthy to do so, and eating in their fallen state would have left them in their sins eternally (Alma 42:4–5).

But make no mistake, Heavenly Father always intended to bring Adam and Eve back to His presence to partake of the tree of life. To do so, Adam and Eve and all of their posterity (ourselves included) would need to be worthy. We would all need to be cleansed (Moses 6:59–62). We all need help through our own modern-day Gardens of Eden, full of trees of knowledge of good and evil—and serpents. We would need a Savior from sin, which is the spiritual death of separation from God. We also need a Redeemer from the physical death, which is the separation of our mortal bodies and eternal spirits, now guaranteed to come on all of us.

To bring about every blessing enjoyed by Adam and Eve before the Fall, God provided the Savior and Redeemer, Jesus Christ, just as set forth in the Grand Council in Heaven (Abraham 3; Moses 4:1–4). To give us access to those blessings of the Savior's Atonement, Heavenly Father followed the eternal pattern and principle of covenant.

In the Old Testament, redemptive commandments and covenants were given to Adam and Eve immediately after the Fall. Moses and the children of Israel received the Mosaic law and what could be properly called the Mosaic covenant. This was the schoolmaster to bring the children of Israel to Christ (Galatians 3:24). King David, who later united Israel, was given a covenant of kingship (2 Samuel 7; Psalm 89; 132).

And of course, Abraham was given the broadest covenant of all in the Old Testament, encompassing the priesthood, the promised land, and posterity without number. Moreover, Abraham's covenant was not just for him but also for all of his posterity (Hebrews 8:8; 12:24; D&C 76:69; 84:57; 107:19). In fact, the terms *Old Testament* and *New Testament* may be correctly translated as *Old Covenant* and *New Covenant*. Both testaments—both covenants—serve to teach and bless the Father's children.

In our day, the Father blesses His children through the new and everlasting covenant, which is the restored gospel of Jesus Christ in its entirety.

The periods of apostasy, when the gospel fulness and the priesthood have been taken from the earth, may appropriately be described as periods of covenant rejection. In simple terms, divine laws were not kept, and the prophets who revealed those laws were rejected. As a result, the blessings associated with those laws were withdrawn. Covenants were broken. Apostasy took their place (Isaiah 24:5).

As we will see, the Abrahamic covenant was the grandest and most comprehensive of all Old Testament covenants. It includes and subsumes all other covenants given in the Old Testament. It restores and expands the blessings of Eden, effectively reversing the effects of the Fall. In our day, its blessings represent the pinnacle of the restored gospel, the new and everlasting covenant on earth today.

## Essential Parts of Biblical Covenants

Understanding the specific characteristics and aspects of biblical covenants is essential to a proper understanding of the covenants we as Latter-day Saints make when we receive the saving ordinances of the gospel.[10] Biblical scholars Kevin Conner and Ken Malmin taught that these biblical covenants in general include essential and specific components.[11] They are:

1. *The promises of the covenant.* These may take the form of both blessings and cursings. They come from God and represent His action in the covenant—His blessings poured out to us through the covenant. Latter-day Saints are familiar with this component. This has not changed from the Old Testament to the latter days.

2. *The terms of the covenant.* These are the conditions that must be fulfilled to receive the promises. They represent our actions. They are the commandments or the sacrifice of the covenant. Commandments and sacrifices are closely linked, as keeping a commandment is itself a sacrifice. Between the promises and terms of the covenant, we see the same pattern discussed earlier: keep a commandment or make a sacrifice, and then receive a promised blessing. This principle and aspect of covenants is eternal. It has not changed from the Old Testament to the Restoration.

3. *The oath of the covenant.* This is a solemn affirmation, with an appeal to God for its truth. For example, a witness in court must swear an oath to tell the truth, the whole truth, and nothing but the truth before testifying. The familiar phrase *so help me God* often accompanies such an oath. In this example, the oath governs the promise to tell the truth, the testimony given pursuant to that promise, and the consequence of the judgment of God if the oath is broken. According to Conner and Malmin, an oath confirms the covenant and makes its terms irrevocable and unchangeable.[12]

   Latter-day Saints are largely familiar with the word *oath* as part of the covenant of the priesthood found in Doctrine and Covenants 84. However, we do not swear formal verbal oaths to accompany many of the gospel covenants we make. In many instances, we instead make affirmations in interviews and attest to our priesthood leaders that we are worthy to participate in ordinances that accompany the covenants. Our verbal participation in some ordinances and covenants is limited to a simple "amen," attesting our agreement with the covenant and ordinance.

Likewise, the ordinances that accompany gospel covenants such as baptism serve as a symbolic oath on our part. For example, Alma taught that the ordinance of baptism served "as a witness before" God of the covenant to serve Him and keep His commandments (Mosiah 18:10). This has not changed from the Old Testament, as the Pearl of Great Price teaches us that the ordinance of baptism has been on the earth from the beginning (Moses 6:64–67).

In Abraham's experience, it is the Lord who swore an oath, sealing the blessings promised to Abraham when he proved his dedication to serving God at all costs (Genesis 22:16). This has not changed in latter days. The requirement of an oath in latter-day covenants has not changed, though some oaths accompanying some covenants may now take a different form than they did anciently.

4. *The blood of the covenant.* Biblical covenants were viewed as life-and-death commitments, so it was appropriate to memorialize and ratify covenants through some form of bloodshed. "The sacrificial blood used to make the covenant official represented the life commitment of those entering into the covenant."[13] Slaying an innocent animal by shedding its blood would be a startling experience, sure to grab the attention of those who worship. It would be a deep and poignant lesson on the nature of covenants and the prophesied sacrifice of the Savior. We don't offer such sacrifices any more, but we would do well to value our covenants as matters of life and death, as represented by blood sacrifices. This "blood of the covenant" is further broken down:

   **The sacrifice of the covenant.** In the Old Testament, an animal sacrifice frequently accompanied covenants. This was done to emphasize the life-and-death nature, the absolute importance of the covenant. With His mortal ministry, the Savior fulfilled the Old Testament law and ended such sacrifice (3 Nephi 9:19). Instead of animal sacrifices, the Lord now requires of us a more subtle and less dramatic—yet somehow more significant—sacrifice: a broken heart and a contrite spirit (3 Nephi 9:20). This is still a blood sacrifice in a real but symbolic way, as it is an offering of the heart, through which all blood passes and the symbolic center of true desire (Mosiah 5:2). Because this sacrifice begins inside of us and is personal, it isn't nearly as dramatic as the slaying of an innocent animal.

Latter-day Saints are therefore not as familiar with the blood aspect of sacrifices. It still exists in latter-day covenants, but it is more symbolic. Whereas Old Testament sacrifices were a blood sacrifice accompanied by death, the sacrifices ordained by the Savior when He fulfilled that law are blood sacrifices of life. The Lamb of God suffered death for us that we might have life. Our lives, reflected and symbolized by a broken heart and a contrite spirit, are the symbolic blood sacrifice we offer to accompany our covenants.

The Savior taught and fulfilled this same blood covenant concept to His disciples when He instituted the sacrament just before His betrayal. "And he took bread, and gave thanks, and brake it, and gave unto them, saying, This is my body which is given for you: this do in remembrance of me. Likewise also the cup after supper, saying, This cup is the new testament in my blood, which is shed for you" (Luke 22:19–20). We now partake of the sacrament to renew our covenants and promise anew that we will always remember Him and keep His commandments. The bread is torn just as the flesh of the sacrifice was torn, and the water is then taken in remembrance of the spilled blood. In the Old Testament, the blood of the sacrifice was literal, which foreshadowed the blood literally shed in Gethsemane and on Golgotha. The blood accompanying the sacrament and other covenants is now more symbolic.

The blood aspect of covenants has changed in the latter-days as a direct result of the Savior's teachings to His disciples and to the Nephites. It is still present in the restored gospel, just now more symbolically so.

**The mediator of the covenant.** Anciently, this person was the priesthood holder who offered the sacrifice and officiated at the sacrifice. Latter-day Saints are familiar with the requirement for a priesthood holder to authorize and officiate ordinances. This priesthood holder symbolically represents Jesus Christ, who is the "mediator of the new covenant" (D&C 76:69; 107:19). This aspect of covenant making has not changed from the Old Testament to the Restoration.

**The sanctuary of the covenant.** This is the sacred space where a covenant is entered into. Conner and Malmin listed two such sanctuaries: an altar and the temple (including the tabernacle of Moses). Latter-day Saints are familiar with sanctuaries, both altars and temples. This aspect of covenants has not changed with the Restoration.

**The seal of the covenant.** This is a tangible witness of the covenant. Conner and Malmin used two other words to reflect a "seal" of the covenant: *sign* and *token*. These two words are significant to Latter-day Saints from Brigham Young's description of the endowment in the temple. "Your endowment is, to receive all those ordinances in the House of the Lord, which are necessary for you, after you have departed this life, to enable you to walk back to the presence of the Father, passing the angels who stand as sentinels, being enabled to give them the key words, the signs and tokens pertaining to the Holy Priesthood, and gain your eternal exaltation in spite of earth and hell."[14] This quote provides the perfect context for understanding signs and tokens as they relate to covenants. The signs and tokens are tangible witnesses of the covenant; they are physical proof of the covenant possessed and cared for by the parties to the covenant.

As a tangible witness or physical proof of the covenant, an ordinance qualifies as a seal, sign, or token of the covenant. An ordinance is a physical act accompanying a covenant, designed to impress on our minds and hearts the covenant we are making. According to Brigham Young's quote, this aspect of covenants has not changed with the Restoration.

In the Abrahamic covenant, we see all of these covenant aspects. They are important to learn and recognize, as they individually and collectively teach great and important spiritual lessons of the covenant. "Therefore, in the ordinances thereof, the power of godliness is manifest" (D&C 84:20).

- *The principle of covenants is eternal. Heavenly Father has used the same pattern of blessing His children through covenants since the Creation.*
- *Beginning with the "Edenic covenant" given to Adam and Eve, the Lord has continued to give other covenants to people throughout the Bible as a means of blessing them and reversing the effects of the Fall.*
- *The Abrahamic covenant is the greatest and most comprehensive of the Old Testament covenants, as it extends to the latter days. The Old Testament covenants, in particular the Abrahamic covenant, literally restore us to the condition before the Fall.*
- *Biblical covenants all include certain specific components that jointly comprise the covenant. These components are still found in the covenants and ordinances of the restored gospel and are particularly helpful in understanding latter-day covenants and the Abrahamic covenant.*
- *The blessings of the Abrahamic covenant—broadly classified as posterity, priesthood, and promised land—are the words of the covenant. They are the Lord's promises to us through it.*
- *The commandments to obey the word of the Lord, follow Him, offer sacrifices, walk before God, be perfect, and sacrifice all that we have are the terms of the covenant. They are the commandments to us and are our promises to the Lord in the covenant.*
- *The oath and sacrifice of this covenant are found in the ordinances that accompany it.*
- *The mediator of this covenant is the holder of the priesthood keys, or the one authorized to administer and officiate in the ordinances of the covenant. Jesus Christ is the ultimate mediator of the covenant.*
- *The sanctuary of the covenant is the temple.*
- *The seal, or tokens and signs of the covenant, is the physical proof of entering into the covenant. Tokens and signs are found in the ordinances that accompany them.*

# Section Two

## The Blessings of the Abrahamic Covenant

**W*e now have*** an understanding of the prevalence and importance of the Abrahamic covenant in the scriptures. We also have an understanding of biblical covenants that adds much to our appreciation of the essential covenants in the Church and the sacred ordinances that accompany them. We now turn to the blessings of the Abrahamic covenant, also called the promises of the covenant, in the context of biblical covenants.

The first and most essential lesson for us to learn on this subject is that these blessings have been restored; they are ours. This is one of the great foundations of the gospel, taught in part by the Savior's parable of the prodigal son. "Son, thou art ever with me, and all that I have is thine" (Luke 15:31). If Abraham is truly our father, then his blessings are our blessings. Their application in our lives will require us to liken the scriptures to our own circumstances (1 Nephi 19:23). These are not just ancient promises to an aging prophet; they are promises to us and ours to claim.

Adam and Eve are our exemplars in the account of the Creation and the Fall. We have been taught throughout the scriptures and the temple endowment that we are to follow their path back to the tree of life, back to the presence of Heavenly Father. Abraham and Sarah are our exemplars in the covenant that paves the way for our ultimate return to God's presence.

In Doctrine and Covenants 132, the Lord pronounced the greatest of all blessings upon the Prophet Joseph Smith—sealing on him the blessings of exaltation (D&C 132:49–50). Those are the fulfilled blessings of the Abrahamic covenant (D&C 132:30–31). In that section, the Lord continually referred to Abraham as an example. To Joseph and to all of us, the Lord invited, "Go ye, therefore, and do the works of Abraham" (D&C 132:32). Abraham and Sarah are therefore our examples in seeking and receiving the greatest blessings the Lord can bestow in mortality.

Another theme to keep in mind is that the blessings of the Abrahamic covenant pertain to both mortality and eternity. Many of these blessings are to be enjoyed in this life, and many of those same blessings overflow into the next. At the same time, some blessings, while promised in mortality, may not be fulfilled in mortality, rather awaiting us in the eternities.

The Lord described the blessings of righteousness as "peace in this world, and eternal life in the world to come" (D&C 59:23). This is especially true of the Abrahamic covenant. These blessings represent, quite literally, the best of both worlds.

# Abraham 1

## Abraham Seeks the Blessings of the Fathers

**L*atter-day Saints have*** several distinct advantages in understanding the Abrahamic covenant. The Pearl of Great Price (specifically the book of Abraham) and the Joseph Smith Translation of the Bible are immensely helpful aids in understanding the Abrahamic covenant. We also have the temple, where the ordinances of the Abrahamic covenant are received. And we have inspired words of the Lord's latter-day servants. In all of these, we have Joseph Smith and the Restoration to thank for all of these blessings in understanding one of the most common and prevalent themes in the scriptures.

This study begins in Abraham 1. This chapter predates the Genesis account and gives us valuable insight into the covenant blessings that first appear in Genesis 12. Abraham 1 reveals the background of the covenant from the perspective of Abraham's desires to receive its blessings.

### The Patriarchal Order of the Priesthood

This lesson starts even before the text of the scripture. The headnote to Abraham 1 teaches straightway, "Abraham seeks the blessings of the patriarchal order." This patriarchal order is essential to understand. To Abraham, the patriarchal order represented both the blessings and the means to receive those blessings. To us today, it represents the same, except that we use different terminology. Instead of overtly saying that we're seeking the blessings of the patriarchal order, we simply say that we're going to the temple. As we study Abraham's story, we will grow to understand the temple much better by learning more of the patriarchal order.

One of the main points in the previous chapter was an understanding that many terms (such as *Israel*) found throughout the scriptures are references to the Abrahamic covenant. One of the most familiar of these references is the prophecy of Elijah's return. It is critical to our understanding of the patriarchal order that Abraham sought. "Behold, I will reveal unto you the Priesthood, by the hand of Elijah the prophet, before the coming of the great and dreadful day of the Lord. And he shall plant in the hearts of the children the promises made to the fathers, and the hearts of the children shall turn to their fathers. If it were not so, the whole earth would be utterly wasted at his coming" (D&C 2:1–3).

This section was received as a promise and a prophecy in September 1823. Even though it appears as the second section of the Doctrine and Covenants, it was actually received some eight years before the first section. In other words, it was actually the first chapter of revelation received in modern scripture. That tells us how important it is to the Lord.

So what is this "Priesthood," without which the "whole earth" would be "utterly wasted"?[15]

Doctrine and Covenants 107 teaches, "There are, in the church, two priesthoods, namely, the Melchizedek and Aaronic, including the Levitical Priesthood" (D&C 107:1). John the Baptist appeared to Joseph Smith and Oliver Cowdery and restored the Aaronic Priesthood in May 1829, as recorded in section 13. Peter, James, and John appeared sometime shortly thereafter to restore the Melchizedek Priesthood. Neither of these priesthoods was restored by the hand of Elijah. He did not come until April 3, 1836, as recorded in section 110.

If Elijah did not restore either of the two priesthoods in the Church, the Aaronic or Melchizedek, what was this "Priesthood" revealed and restored by him? It was the patriarchal authority, also known as the patriarchal order, patriarchal priesthood, or (unofficially) the Abrahamic priesthood.[16]

Elder Theodore M. Burton taught,

> With this fulfillment of prophecy [of the coming of Elijah], all former priesthood powers were restored again to earth. Temples have been erected in which a fulness of these priesthood ordinances is made available for those who qualify themselves to receive them through faith and righteous living. Before the Savior comes again, power has been given us to proceed with a great priesthood work. We are to bind together the families of men in true *patriarchal order*, so that through worthiness we may have the privilege to live in the celestial kingdom as children of God, with resurrected bodies of flesh and bone, to dwell eternally in the very presence of God the Eternal Father.[17]

How does this patriarchal order, or patriarchal priesthood, fit in with the Aaronic and Melchizedek Priesthoods? Eight years after receiving Doctrine and Covenants 107, Joseph Smith taught, "There are three grand orders of the priesthood referred to" in Hebrews 7. The first of these is the Melchizedek Priesthood. Joseph Smith said further,

> What was the power of Melchizedek? 'Twas not the Priesthood of Aaron which administers in outward ordinances, and the offering of sacrifices. *Those holding the fulness of the Melchizedek Priesthood are kings and priests of the most High God, holding the keys of power and blessings.* In fact, that Priesthood is a perfect law of theocracy, and stands as God to give laws to the people, administering endless lives to the sons and daughters of Adam.[18]

Joseph Smith then prefaced his statement on the second "grand order of the priesthood," stating,

> Salvation could not come to the world without the mediation of Jesus Christ.
>
> How shall God come to the rescue of this generation? He will send Elijah the prophet. The law revealed to Moses in Horeb never was revealed to the children as a nation. Elijah shall reveal the covenants to seal the hearts of the fathers to the children, and the children to the fathers.
>
> The anointing and sealing is to be called, elected and made sure.

"Without father, without mother, without descent, having neither beginning of days nor end of life, but made like unto the Son of God, abideth a priest continually." The Melchizedek Priesthood holds the right from the eternal God, and not by descent from father and mother; and that priesthood is as eternal as God Himself, having neither beginning of days nor end of life.

The [second] Priesthood is Patriarchal authority. Go to and finish the temple, and God will fill it with power, and you will then receive more knowledge concerning this priesthood.[19]

Joseph then taught that the third order is the familiar Aaronic, or Levitical, Priesthood, whose functions of sacrifice and outward ordinances were given in his explanation of the Melchizedek Priesthood.[20]

To help harmonize these statements, Elder Boyd K. Packer taught,

> There are references to a patriarchal priesthood. The patriarchal order is not a third, separate priesthood. . . . Whatever relates to the patriarchal order is embraced in the Melchizedek Priesthood. "All other authorities or offices in the church are appendages to [the Melchizedek] priesthood" (D&C 107:5). The patriarchal order is a part of the Melchizedek Priesthood which enables endowed and worthy men to preside over their posterity in time and eternity.[21]

This same patriarchal order, or patriarchal priesthood, is sometimes unofficially referred to as the "Abrahamic Priesthood" because it is the order of the priesthood that governs and pertains to the administration of the Abrahamic covenant. Neither this priesthood nor its ordinances and blessings originated with Abraham, just as the Melchizedek Priesthood did not originate with Melchizedek. Still, we correctly refer to the covenant as the Abrahamic covenant because of Abraham's role and example.

Just as Adam and Eve are our exemplars in the account of the Creation and the Fall, Abraham and Sarah are our exemplars in the covenant that completely reverses the effects of the Fall and brings Adam and Eve's posterity back into the presence of God.

Putting these prophetic declarations together, we learn:

- There is the Aaronic, or Levitical, Priesthood, which is a preparatory priesthood used to administer in sacrifices and the outward ordinances of the gospel.

- There is the Melchizedek Priesthood. The fulness of this priesthood holds the keys of being kings and priests.
- Within the Melchizedek Priesthood, there is the patriarchal order. This order (meaning division or substructure) is sometimes called the patriarchal priesthood, or (unofficially) the Abrahamic Priesthood. It is specific to the functions of the temple. This is the "Priesthood" restored by Elijah.

## Other Titles and References to This Priesthood Order

As is evident from Joseph Smith's description of the endowment, the patriarchal order has many other sacred titles that also teach of its history, sacredness, and purposes.

*The order of the Son of God.* President Ezra Taft Benson in particular spoke beautifully on this, the temple, and the blessings of Abraham. In doing so, he chose two other titles to describe this order. In titling his address "What I Hope You Will Teach Your Children about the Temple," President Benson's prophetic invitation is that we, as members of the Church who have received these temple blessings, teach our children and impart to them an understanding of these same blessings.

> I believe a proper understanding or background will immeasurably help prepare our youth for the temple. This understanding, I believe, will foster within them a desire to seek their priesthood blessings just as Abraham sought his.
>
> When our Heavenly Father placed Adam and Eve on this earth, He did so with the purpose in mind of teaching them how to regain His presence. Our Father promised a Savior to redeem them from their fallen condition. He gave to them the plan of salvation and told them to teach their children faith in Jesus Christ and repentance. Further, Adam and his posterity were commanded by God to be baptized, to receive the Holy Ghost, and to enter into the order of the Son of God.
>
> To enter into the order of the Son of God is the equivalent today of entering into the fulness of the Melchizedek Priesthood, which is only received in the house of the Lord.[22]

Here, President Benson cited another title for the patriarchal order: the order of the Son of God. This title comes from Moses 6:67, which says, "And thou art after the order of him who was without beginning of days or end of years, from all eternity to all eternity." This reference to the Son of God and the order named after Him comes following Adam's baptism, a prerequisite ordinance for entering into this order.

*The fulness of the Melchizedek Priesthood.* In the previous quotation, President Benson also spoke of entering into the fulness of the Melchizedek Priesthood, "which is only received in the house of the Lord." Whereas this order was called "the order of the Son of God" anciently, its latter-day equivalent is "the fulness of the Melchizedek Priesthood."

Doctrine and Covenants 76 uses the same word—*fulness*—among several other significant and sacred words to describe the glory of the celestial kingdom (see Doctrine and Covenants 76:20). This is no coincidence. The blessings of the celestial kingdom—the fulness of the Father—are only reached through the priesthood and the temple.

Notice how this section of scripture lists the gospel ordinances and covenants that lead to the fulness.

> They are they who received the testimony of Jesus, and believed on his name and were baptized after the manner of his burial, being buried in the water in his name, and this according to the commandment which he has given—
>
> That by keeping the commandments they might be washed and cleansed from all their sins, and receive the Holy Spirit by the laying on of the hands of him who is ordained and sealed unto this power;
>
> And who overcome by faith, and are sealed by the Holy Spirit of promise, which the Father sheds forth upon all those who are just and true.
>
> They are they who are the church of the Firstborn.
>
> They are they into whose hands the Father has given all things—
>
> They are they who are priests and kings, who have received of his fulness, and of his glory;
>
> And are priests of the Most High, after the order of Melchizedek, which was after the order of Enoch, which was after the order of the Only Begotten Son.
>
> Wherefore, as it is written, they are gods, even the sons of God. . . .

> These are they who are come unto Mount Zion, and unto the city of the living God, the heavenly place, the holiest of all.
>
> These are they who have come to an innumerable company of angels, to the general assembly and church of Enoch, and of the Firstborn. (D&C 76:51–58, 66–67)

In this revelation, the word *fulness* falls in the middle of the most significant and sacred blessings bestowed on those who live a celestial law and inherit an eternal celestial glory. The ordinances and covenants of the gospel pave that way.

These ordinances and covenants are administered only through the Melchizedek Priesthood, even the same fulness of the priesthood, as stated by President Benson. "The power and authority of the higher, or Melchizedek Priesthood, is to hold the keys of all the spiritual blessings of the church—to have the privilege of receiving the mysteries of the kingdom of heaven, to have the heavens opened unto them, to commune with the general assembly and church of the Firstborn, and to enjoy the communion and presence of God the Father, and Jesus the mediator of the new covenant" (D&C 107:18–19).

This scripture is staggering in the scale of Melchizedek Priesthood blessings that it describes. The Aaronic Priesthood holds the keys of the ministering of angels and the gospel of repentance and baptism (see Doctrine and Covenants 13). The Melchizedek Priesthood holds the keys to even higher blessings: revelation, mysteries of the kingdom of heaven, and eternal life.

As we read before, section 76 describes the celestial kingdom in terms of blessings and qualifications. The reference in section 107 describes more such blessings while stating the power and authority that leads to them. The fulness of the priesthood necessarily refers to these blessings, as they are administered through the keys of the Melchizedek Priesthood.

## The Fulness of the Priesthood and the Temple

Joseph Smith taught, "If a man gets a fulness of the priesthood of God he has to get it in the same way that Jesus Christ obtained it, and that was by keeping all the commandments and obeying all the ordinances of the house of the Lord."[23]

Doctrine and Covenants 124 also uses this same significant word—*fulness*—in connection with the temple. As Joseph Smith taught, the temple is the place where the fulness of blessings is unlocked and the fulness of the priesthood is exercised. In commanding the Saints to "build a house" to the Lord's name "for the Most High to dwell therein," the Lord immediately declared, "For there is not a place found on earth that he may come to and restore again that which was lost unto you, or which he hath taken away, even the fulness of the priesthood" (D&C 124:27–28).

In section 124, we see that the Melchizedek Priesthood encompasses the patriarchal order of the priesthood, also called the fulness of the priesthood. This priesthood order leads to a fulness of eternal blessings and glory, found only in the ordinances and covenants of the temple.

No doubt the scriptures have many other "fulness" references that pertain to the blessings and ordinances of the Abrahamic covenant in the temple.

## The Patriarchal Order and Joseph Smith's Description of the Endowment

The connection between the patriarchal order and the ordinances of the temple becomes more evident in Joseph Smith's description of the endowment. Much of what we now recognize as the temple endowment ceremony was restored through Joseph Smith and administered in the upper floor of Joseph's red brick store in Nauvoo on May 4, 1842. Just three days before, Joseph wrote in his journal,

> I preached in the grove, on the keys of the kingdom, charity, &c. The keys are certain signs and words by which false spirits and personages may be detected from true, which cannot be revealed to the Elders till the Temple is completed. The rich can only get them in the Temple, the poor may get them on the mountain top as did Moses. The rich cannot be saved without charity, giving to feed the poor when and how God requires, as well as building. There are signs in heaven, earth and hell; the Elders must know them all, to be endowed with power,

> to finish their work and prevent imposition. The devil knows many signs, but does not know the sign of the Son of Man, or Jesus. No one can truly say he knows God until he has handled something, and this can only be in the holiest of holies.[24]

Then, on that great day of May 4, Joseph's journal entry for that day reads,

> I spent the day in the upper part of the store, that is in my private office (so called because in that room I keep my sacred writings, translate ancient records, and receive revelations) and in my general business office, or lodge room (that is where the Masonic fraternity meet occasionally, for want of a better place) in council with General James Adams, of Springfield, Patriarch Hyrum Smith, Bishops Newel K. Whitney and George Miller, and President Brigham Young and Elders Heber C. Kimball and Willard Richards, instructing them in the principles and *order of the Priesthood*, attending to washings, anointing, endowments and the communication of keys pertaining to the Aaronic Priesthood, and so on to *the highest order of the Melchisedek Priesthood*, setting for *the order pertaining to the Ancient of Days*, and all those plans and principles by which any one is enabled to secure the fulness of those blessings which have been prepared for the Church of the First Born, and we come up and abide in the presence of the Eloheim in the eternal worlds. In this council was instituted *the ancient order of things* for the first time in these last days. And the communications I made to this council were of things spiritual, and to be received only by the spiritual minded: and there was nothing made known to these men but what will be made known to all the Saints of the last days, so soon as they are prepared to receive, and a proper place is prepared to communicate them, even to the weakest of the Saints; therefore let the Saints be diligent in building the Temple, and all houses which they have been, or shall hereafter be, commanded of God to build; and wait their time with patience in all meekness, faith, perseverance unto the end, knowing assuredly that all these things referred to in this council are always governed by the principle of revelation.[25]

Tying these two quotes together, Joseph spoke first of "signs," and he then spoke of the endowment. The two are inseparable. In the chapter on biblical covenants, we learned that signs, tokens, and seals were used anciently as the physical evidence and proof of a covenant.

As such, a sign or token is far more than a simple word, action, or object; it is a symbol or an emblem of proof of deep and eternal significance. It represents the covenant itself. So, when Joseph spoke of signs, the real message was the covenant and the priesthood behind that sign.

Brigham Young described the same experience in words that are perhaps more familiar to us, referenced previously. He also spoke of "signs" and of receiving "all those ordinances in the House of the Lord" that enable us to "walk back to the presence of the Father, passing the angels who stand as sentinels, being enabled to give them the key words, the signs and tokens pertaining to the Holy Priesthood, and gain [our] eternal exaltation in spite of earth and hell."[26]

Both Brigham and Joseph were describing the same temple experience. Both spoke of key words and signs related to the priesthood. Joseph taught that these keys belonged to both the Aaronic and the Melchizedek Priesthoods, specifically mentioning the highest order of the Melchizedek Priesthood. Both taught that these ordinances enable us to return to the presence of the Father. Both taught that these ordinances and the signs (or covenants) accompanying them are received only in the temple. Of course, the mere act of entering into the covenant doesn't entitle anyone to salvation or exaltation. The covenant must be kept, not just made. Therefore, both prophets used the word *signs* to refer broadly to temple covenants made and kept.

Joseph's and Brigham's descriptions differ perhaps most notably in that Joseph's 1842 statement refers to these blessings four separate times in terms of an "order." All of these refer to the same patriarchal order that Abraham sought.

Our modern-day prophets, beginning with Joseph Smith's original description of the endowment, have taught that receiving the ordinances of the temple means entering into the patriarchal order. In seeking the blessings of the patriarchal order, Abraham was seeking the blessings of the temple.

## The Patriarchal Order of the Priesthood and the Oath and Covenant of the Priesthood

The oath and covenant of the priesthood is also a reflection of the patriarchal order. Those who are "faithful unto the obtaining these two priesthoods . . . and the magnifying their calling, are sanctified by the Spirit unto the renewing of their bodies. They become the sons of Moses and of Aaron and the seed of Abraham, and the church and kingdom, and the elect of God" (D&C 84:33–34). The "seed of Abraham" refers, of course, to those who receive the Abrahamic covenant. As we have seen, that means those who receive the ordinances of the patriarchal order in the temple.

"And also all they who receive this priesthood receive me, saith the Lord" (D&C 84:35). In the previous verses, the Lord spoke of "these two priesthoods"—plural—meaning the Aaronic and Melchizedek. In this verse, the Lord spoke of a singular priesthood. One explanation for this transition from plural to singular is that the Lord was referring to the priesthood of the "seed of Abraham," meaning the highest order of the priesthood, which is administered under the Melchizedek Priesthood.

The promises of the next several verses support this thought. "For he that receiveth my servants receiveth me; and he that receiveth me receiveth my Father; and he that receiveth my Father receiveth my Father's kingdom; therefore all that my Father hath shall be given unto him" (D&C 84:36–38). This promise from the Lord is an assurance that we can receive all that the Father hath. The priesthood that provides for such infinite blessings is the Abrahamic Priesthood, the patriarchal order of the priesthood.

It is not the mere act of receiving any priesthood that entitles someone to these highest blessings; it is making and keeping the covenants and ordinances pertaining to this highest order of the priesthood that has the power to bestow the highest blessings. Mere ordination to either of the priesthoods does not confer all that the Father hath. Those blessings are the fulness of the Father. They can only be found in the temple through the patriarchal order of the priesthood.

As an Apostle, President Joseph Fielding Smith taught this same truth. "So being ordained an elder, or a high priest, or an apostle, or even president of the Church, is not the thing that brings exaltation, but obedience to the laws and the ordinances and the covenants required of those who desire to become members of the Church of the Firstborn, as these are administered in the House of the Lord."[27] The true essence of the oath and covenant of the priesthood isn't simply ordination to the Aaronic Priesthood or Melchizedek Priesthood. The true essence is the "Priesthood" (D&C 2:1), which is administered in the temple and leads to the fulness of the Lord's blessings.

Generally speaking, when you read or hear the word *fulness* in the context of the gospel, it is a reference to the temple and its ordinances—the ordinances of the fulness of the Lord.

## The Patriarchal Order in Our Everyday Lives

One of the most profound and practical lessons I have learned on the patriarchal order came without any fanfare or overt references to the temple. It came from a journal entry from President Henry B. Eyring when he was president of Ricks College (now BYU–Idaho), as recorded in his biography. The journal entry reflects the goals of the Church's education leaders over the ten years following 1971. President Eyring wrote,

> The Select Committee meeting was an unusual blend of fresh, divergent thinking, sparked by disagreement, yet a feeling of the Spirit leading and shaping the discussion. That's amazing, with 20 strong men in the group. To my surprise, near the end of the three hours before lunch, we agreed that a reasonable question to pursue is "If we looked at a 10-year planning horizon and assumed the Lord would come then, what behaviors, attitudes, and skills would the members of the Church and those around them need to have for the Lord to be able come?" Here are just some of the answers:
>
> The patriarchal order working well enough in most homes that the present auxiliary functions could be performed in the home.[28]

This reflects the true purpose of the patriarchal order. Adam and Eve gathered their posterity anciently and taught them the truths of the gospel of Jesus Christ. In doing this, they were living the patriarchal order. We cannot afford to think of the patriarchal order as an esoteric subject, or even strictly as a temple doctrine. The purpose and function of the order are for us to take the lessons and covenants of the temple to our homes and our callings and teach those within our stewardships. That is the essence of the patriarchal order: a husband and wife united in their devotion to the Lord and teaching the gospel by precept (meaning face-to-face, one-on-one) and example every day. The temple is where we *enter* into the patriarchal order, and the home is primarily where we *live* the patriarchal order.

## Summary

In seeking the "blessings of the fathers" (Abraham 1:2), or the blessings of the patriarchal order of the priesthood, Abraham was seeking the ordinances of the temple. These ordinances alone have the power to bring the children of Abraham back to the presence of God.

- *Abraham specifically sought the blessings of the patriarchal order. This priesthood order is the backdrop of the Abrahamic covenant.*
- *This patriarchal order exists within the Melchizedek Priesthood and is the highest order of the priesthood.*
- *The patriarchal order governs the ordinances of exaltation, which are found only in the temple.*
- *The patriarchal order is also referred to as the order of the Son of God, the order of God, and the fulness of the Melchizedek Priesthood.*
- *Because this order governs and authorizes the temple ordinances of the Abrahamic covenant, some people have unofficially referred to it as the Abrahamic Priesthood.*
- *The sealing power restored by the prophet Elijah pertains to these ordinances and blessings of the patriarchal order.*
- *Generally speaking, scriptural references to "the fulness" or to "patriarchal" things are references to the same priesthood order and its ordinances and its blessings. Scriptural references to "the fulness" are also references to the temple and its ordinances.*
- *In restoring the temple endowment, Joseph Smith described the blessings of the temple as entering into this highest order of the Melchizedek Priesthood.*

- *The oath and covenant of the priesthood in Doctrine and Covenants 84 and its promise of obtaining "all that the Father hath" are also references to this order of the priesthood.*
- *We live this patriarchal order by being united in teaching the gospel by precept and by example to our families. Of course, this is done primarily in the home.*

# Greater Happiness, Peace, Rest, Knowledge, and Follower of Righteousness

U***nderstanding the patriarchal*** order of the priesthood as Abraham's goal, let's dive into the scriptural account and the other specific details of the blessings Abraham sought.

In the land of the Chaldeans, at the residence of my fathers, I, Abraham, saw that it was needful for me to obtain another place of residence;

And, finding there was greater happiness and peace and rest for me, I sought for the blessings of the fathers, and the right whereunto I should be ordained to administer the same; having been myself a follower of righteousness, desiring also to be one who possessed great knowledge, and to be a greater follower of righteousness, and to possess a greater knowledge, and to be a father of many nations, a prince of peace, and desiring to receive instructions, and to keep the commandments of God, I became a rightful heir, a High Priest, holding the right belonging to the fathers.

It was conferred upon me from the fathers; it came down from the fathers, from the beginning of time, yea, even from the beginning, or before the foundation of the earth, down to the present time, even the right of the firstborn, or the first man, who is Adam, or first father, through the fathers unto me.

> I sought for mine appointment unto the Priesthood according to the appointment of God unto the fathers concerning the seed. (Abraham 1:1–4)

Several words and phrases in this passage are worth looking into further.

*It was needful for me to obtain another place of residence.* We learn from this that Abraham came from a lineage that should have blessed him with this priesthood he was seeking, but his father had fallen into idolatry. The Pearl of Great Price teaches that these wicked practices of idolatry threatened Abraham's life, even to the point where he was going to be sacrificed to a false god. (Divine intervention ultimately spared him.)

The modern Chaldea in which you and I live also requires us to leave. Entering into the covenant waters of baptism requires us symbolically to leave the Chaldea or Babylon that surrounds us and move toward Zion. We may not literally move to a new address, but we most definitely separate ourselves from the community where false gods are worshipped as we draw near to the God of Abraham, Isaac, and Jacob.

*Greater.* With the understanding that Abraham was seeking the patriarchal order of the priesthood, verse two gives a wealth of insights into the blessings pertaining to the order. The word *greater* makes several important appearances in Abraham's story. Verse two begins with Abraham seeking "greater happiness and peace and rest." Those three blessings appear as one, not separated by any comma or other punctuation. They are inseparable in Abrahamic terms.

Verse two also speaks of Abraham's desire to be a "greater follower of righteousness" and to possess "a greater knowledge." The repeated use of the word *greater* brings to mind the word *fulness,* used so frequently to teach of the blessings of the Abrahamic covenant. Abraham was already a follower of righteousness and already had knowledge. He simply wanted more. He wanted a fulness.

Abraham had already enjoyed the blessings of the gospel and the blessings of happiness, peace, and rest. Like many of us, he received those blessings when he received the introductory ordinances of the gospel and lived the laws that accompany them. Abraham specifically sought those same blessings, just in greater quality and quantity.

He recognized the blessings of the fathers, received through the patriarchal order of the priesthood, as the means to receiving those blessings. The ultimate happiness, peace, and rest are found in eternal life. It is easy to lose track of these goals when we are surrounded by modern-day Chaldeans, but Abraham's desires are a reminder of the blessings of those who truly want more. The "greater" blessings of the gospel are found in the higher ordinances of the gospel.

*A father of many nations.* Among the blessings Abraham sought were the blessings of posterity. Though we have referred to him as "Abraham" throughout, his name at this point in his life was actually "Abram." Abram means "exalted father," quite a flattering and holy name in itself. Abram later received a new name that also reflects the blessing of posterity that he sought.

*A prince of peace.* Abraham sought to become a prince of peace, a title applied to the Savior Himself. Isaiah prophesied of Christ's birth and mission using this exact term. "For unto us a child is born, unto us a son is given: and the government shall be upon his shoulder: and his name shall be called Wonderful, Counsellor, The mighty God, The everlasting Father, The Prince of Peace" (Isaiah 9:6). Abraham wasn't seeking to take honor or glory from the Son of God by usurping His title; quite the contrary, Abraham wanted to follow the example of the Son. That is the Savior's invitation to all, and Abraham took this charge quite seriously.

Remember that one of the titles of the patriarchal order is the order of the Son of God. Abraham's desire to be a "prince of peace" is at least in part a reference to his desire to enter into the order of the Son of God and obtain the higher blessings of the Melchizedek Priesthood, which we are told was also originally named after the Son of God (D&C 107:2–4).

Another possibility is that this title foreshadows the promised blessing that *the* Prince of Peace would be born through Abraham's lineage.

*To receive instructions, and to keep the commandments of God.* Abraham's quest "to receive instructions, and to keep the commandments of God" is another temple reference, also from Isaiah. Isaiah's prophecy of the latter-day temple names two specific functions of the mountain of the Lord's house. "And many people shall go and say, Come ye, and let us go up to the mountain of the Lord, to the house of the God of Jacob; and he will teach us of his ways, and we will walk in his paths: for out of Zion shall go forth the law, and the word of the Lord from Jerusalem" (Isaiah 2:3). The two-fold purpose of the temple described by Isaiah is for the Lord to teach His children of His ways and for those being taught to walk in the Lord's path.

Abraham wanted to learn of the Lord's ways. The temple is where divine instruction is received through the ordinances and covenants. The Lord's children then leave the temple under covenant to walk in His ways. Abraham's choice of words in seeking to "receive instructions" and to "keep the commandments of God" (or "walk in" the Lord's ways) is no coincidence. He desired the blessings of the temple, the same blessings carefully chosen and specifically stated as part of Isaiah's temple prophecy.

*A High Priest, holding the right belonging to the fathers.* This is another reference to the patriarchal order of the priesthood that Abraham sought. This priesthood alone holds the keys to the greater blessings of the gospel. It gained its title because it followed a patriarchal pattern, being passed down from righteous father to righteous father, starting with Adam (Abraham 1:3–4). Doctrine and Covenants 107 expounds on this subject. "The order of this priesthood was confirmed to be handed down from father to son, and rightly belongs to the literal descendants of the chosen seed, to whom the promises were made. This order was instituted in the days of Adam, and came down by lineage . . . that his posterity should be the chosen of the Lord, and that they should be preserved unto the end of the earth" (D&C 107:40–42).

In addition to giving the history of this order, section 107 gives an example of it. This section speaks of a magnificent priesthood meeting and family council held by the high priest Adam three years before his death. It was a family council because he gathered all of his family who were worthy to be there (D&C 107:53). It was a priesthood meeting because many of those invited are specifically listed as high priests. In gathering his family, Adam had a specific purpose in this: to bestow "his last blessing." What was the great, last blessing Adam wanted to bestow on his family? He "wanted to bring them into the presence of God."[29]

"How did Adam bring his descendants into the presence of the Lord? . . . [By entering] into the priesthood order of God. Today we would say they went to the house of the Lord and received their blessings."[30]

Here, we have perhaps the greatest lesson we can learn on the patriarchal order of the priesthood: its purpose. The blessings of the temple and the patriarchal order are the blessings of bringing posterity back to the presence of God.

Understanding that the blessings Abraham sought—the blessings of the patriarchal order, or the "blessings of the fathers"—are the blessings of "bringing [Adam's] descendants [back] into the presence of the Lord," we can safely conclude that the ultimate blessings of the temple are the blessings of bringing us as families back to the presence of the Lord. We can also conclude that the most prevalent theme in the scriptures is not simply the Abrahamic covenant, but also its purpose: to bring families back into the presence of God.

## The Patriarchal Order of the Priesthood and Women

Every sealing ordinance of the temple necessarily involves both men and women. Likewise, the blessings of the endowment are for both men and women. These are the ordinances pertaining to the patriarchal order of the priesthood, and it is clear that they are not limited to men. To be clear, women are not ordained to the priesthood, but the patriarchal order of the priesthood is fundamentally open to both the sons of Adam and the daughters of Eve.

Elder Dallin H. Oaks has taught, "Unlike priesthood keys and priesthood ordinations, the blessings of the priesthood are available to women and to men on the same terms. The gift of the Holy Ghost and the blessings of the temple are familiar illustrations of this truth."[31]

Further on this point, Elder M. Russell Ballard said, "When men and women go to the temple, they are both endowed with the same power, which is priesthood power. . . . Access to the power and the blessings of the priesthood is available to all of God's children."[32]

Women are welcome participants in this order of the priesthood; in fact, they are indispensable! There is no patriarch without a matriarch. There is no father in the eternities without a mother in the eternities. The blessings of this priesthood order aren't exclusive to men, but rather are inclusive of men and women. These blessings cannot be realized without women.

On this subject, Archibald Bennett, in an LDS Sunday School manual from the 1950s, taught, "In order to attain to the highest degree of the celestial kingdom, every person must find his place in the celestial family organization. Those who receive this highest reward may become eventually kings and queens, priests and priestesses unto the Most High, and are called gods, even the sons of God."[33] This is a clear and unmistakable reminder that the blessings of this covenant and order of the priesthood are to both men and women.

This quote also gives the titles, if you will, within the patriarchal order of the priesthood, which is administered in the temple. Those titles, including queens and priestesses, are clearly not restricted to men. Understanding and appreciation of these titles will deepen when you contemplate the temple ordinances that lead to these blessings of the priesthood in the Abrahamic covenant.

Expounding deeper on this same subject, Joseph Smith stated,

> Blessed of the Lord is my father, for he shall stand in the midst of his posterity and shall be comforted by their blessings . . . and shall be called a prince over them, . . . for he shall assemble together his posterity like unto Adam; and the assembly which he called shall be an example for my father, . . . and he shall sit in the general assembly of Patriarchs, even in council with the Ancient of Days when he shall sit and all the Patriarchs with him and shall enjoy his right and authority under the direction of the Ancient of Days. And blessed also, is my mother, for she is a mother in Israel, and shall be a partaker with my father in all his patriarchal blessings . . . and thus saith the Lord, She shall have eternal life."[34]

The priesthood doesn't exclude women. To the contrary, the highest order of it exalts women beyond anything this world can bestow or even fathom. This is the order that crowns queens and priestesses for the eternities. In this real sense, the priesthood, in its fulness, is the most ennobling and exalting doctrine for women that God has ever revealed or could ever reveal.

## "Behold, I Will Lead Thee by My Hand"

The backdrop of Abraham 1 continues with a beautiful set of promises to Abraham. In saving Abraham's life from idolaters, including Abraham's own father, the Lord told Abraham, "Behold, I will lead thee by my hand, and I will take thee, to put upon thee my name, even the Priesthood of thy father, and my power shall be over thee. As it was with Noah so shall it be with thee; but through thy ministry my name shall be known in the earth forever, for I am thy god" (Abraham 1:18–19).

These promises give insightful background to the Abrahamic covenant blessings that follow in Abraham 2 and throughout Genesis. It appears to be a promise before the great promises. In this sense, it may prefigure covenants made in the premortal existence. The mortal experience remains indispensable along with its covenants, trials, and heartaches. Still, there is some assurance from a loving Heavenly Father that everything will be fine as we venture into this great unknown. His hand is over us. Stay the course, and we will return to Him.

- *The blessings sought by Abraham—to receive greater blessings, be a father of many nations, be a prince of peace, receive instructions, and keep the commandments of God—are all references to the ordinances and blessings of the temple.*
- *The blessings of the temple are the blessings of greater peace and happiness and rest in our everyday lives, which Abraham sought. In the temple, we also receive the higher ordinances and higher instruction that Abraham desired.*
- *The ultimate purpose of the patriarchal order and meaning of these blessings is quite simply to bring families back to the presence of God. Therefore, we can conclude that the most common theme in the scriptures is not just the Savior and the Abrahamic covenant, but their joint purpose: to bring families back into the presence of the Lord.*

- *Men and women are equal and indispensable partners and participants in this patriarchal order, which is the highest order of the priesthood. This order includes kings, priests, queens, and priestesses.*

# Genesis 12 and Abraham 2

## "Thy Servant Has Sought Thee Earnestly; Now I Have Found Thee"

**The essential background** of the Abrahamic covenant found in Abraham 1 places the Genesis account of Abraham in a whole different light. Abraham 1 teaches us that Abraham was openly and actively seeking the blessings of the fathers, meaning the blessings of the patriarchal order of the priesthood or the blessings of the temple. He was a man of God in search of greater blessings, happiness, peace, rest, and knowledge. He wanted to be an even greater follower of righteousness than he already was, be a prince of peace and a father of many nations, and receive instructions from God and keep His commandments.

Now in Abraham 2, and its counterpart Genesis 12, Abraham found what he had been seeking. The temple experience unfolded in Genesis 12 didn't happen by chance. Abraham had spent his life in search of the blessings promised to him at Haran on his way to Canaan.

Genesis 12 is the first of several chapters where the blessings of the covenant are enumerated and promised to Abraham. It is also the first of several chapters where the Lord gave Abraham specific instructions in connection with those promises. At the time, Abraham was either sixty-two or seventy-six (see Abraham 2:14; Genesis 12:4). When

Abraham received the promises the final time in Genesis 22, he was around 120. Decades have passed. Countless trials have followed with those decades. In this section of Genesis, covering Abraham, Isaac, and Jacob, each chapter spans an average of fourteen years. As is clear, the blessings of this covenant were repeated many times throughout the life of this great patriarch and his sons.

Why are the blessings of the covenant repeated and laid out so many different times over the years? One apparent answer is that the Lord teaches by repetition. The word *remember* is one of the most important in the gospel. The Lord repeated the promises to Abraham in much the same way that He now repeats promises of blessings to us. Our minds are fragile. One bad day is all too often enough to make us forget the blessings we have and those we have been promised. We take the sacrament each week and promise to remember our Savior. Each week when we do so, we hear the same sacrament prayer, as the Lord teaches by repetition. Each time we attend the temple, we hear the same words of the ceremony—repetition.

Many times the important things in life somehow seem less important with continued exposure and repetition. But there is nothing unimportant about the sacrament that is administered with the same prayer and in the same manner every week. There is nothing unimportant about the ceremonies of the temple, which are repeated each time we attend. The repetition in ordinances serves as a much-needed reminder. If the repetition is making the experience seem less important, then we are losing track of the lesson. The Lord taught Abraham by repetition, and we should be grateful that He continues to teach that way throughout our lives.

The repeated promises to Abraham were also a tender mercy to him. No doubt there were many times in those decades when he must have questioned the promises made in Abraham 2 and Genesis 12. As a human—even an extraordinarily righteous human—he must have wondered if he had misunderstood the promises made to him or if he had done something to disqualify himself from those blessings. He had spent decades waiting for the blessings to be fulfilled, and he was still waiting for much of the story to be fulfilled in his old age. Still, he never lost his faith, and his obedience to the Lord never wavered.

## The Blessings to Abraham

*I will make of thee a great nation.* This is the blessing of posterity. It is introduced directly in Genesis with no preface beyond the invitation for Abraham to leave his home and find a new one. This same blessing is renewed in other scriptural accounts. In the next chapter, the Lord expounded on this same promise, comparing Abraham's promised posterity to "the dust of the earth" (Genesis 13:16).

In Abraham 2, the Lord introduced the blessings of the covenant by stating His position as the mediator of the covenant. "For I am the Lord thy God; I dwell in heaven; the earth is my footstool; I stretch my hand over the sea, and it obeys my voice; I cause the wind and the fire to be my chariot; I say to the mountains—Depart hence—and behold, they are taken away by a whirlwind, in an instant, suddenly. My name is Jehovah, and I know the end from the beginning; therefore my hand shall be over thee" (Abraham 2:7–8).

The Lord has followed this pattern of divine introduction throughout the scriptures. In introducing Himself to Moses to declare His plans, the Lord stated, "I am the God of thy father, the God of Abraham, the God of Isaac, and the God of Jacob" (Exodus 3:6). In bestowing the sealing power on the prophet Nephi in the book of Helaman, the Lord said, "Behold, thou art Nephi, and I am God. Behold, I declare it unto thee in the presence of mine angels . . . I give unto you power, that whatsoever ye shall seal on earth shall be sealed in heaven; and whatsoever ye shall loose on earth shall be loosed in heaven" (Helaman 10:6–7). And in pronouncing the same blessing on Joseph Smith in the latter days, the Lord again taught, "For I am the Lord thy God, and will be with thee even unto the end of the world" (D&C 132:49).

The blessing began with Abraham seeking God. Abraham, like all righteous people in ancient and modern times, had to seek God to find Him. The pattern is eternal. We knock, and He opens. We ask, and He reveals Himself (see Doctrine and Covenants 88:63).

*They shall bear this ministry and Priesthood unto all nations.* This is the blessing of priesthood. Not only would Abraham be blessed with great posterity, but his posterity would also hold the priesthood of God and carry the covenant promises to all nations. In other words,

Abraham's posterity would not only be many, they would also be righteous. They would hold the priesthood—the power and authority to act in the name of God to bless His children—and carry it to the rest of the world. They would be the missionaries and the temple workers to bring the truth to the world and the gospel to both sides of the veil. Abraham's descendants, through his great-grandsons Ephraim and Manasseh, primarily held this responsibility.

> And I will bless them through thy name; for as many as receive this Gospel shall be called after thy name, and shall be accounted thy seed, and shall rise up and bless thee, as their father; and I will bless them that bless thee, and curse them that curse thee; and in thee (that is, in thy Priesthood) and in thy seed (that is, thy Priesthood), for I give unto thee a promise that this right shall continue in thee, and in thy seed after thee (that is to say, the literal seed, or the seed of the body) shall all the families of the earth be blessed, even with the blessings of the Gospel, which are the blessings of salvation, even of life eternal. (Abraham 2:10–11)

Notice whom specifically the priesthood of Abraham's posterity will bless; in both the Abraham and the Genesis accounts, it is the families of the earth (Abraham 2:11; Genesis 12:3). The family is the eternal unit of God, and the family will specifically be blessed by the Abrahamic covenant.

Notice also the means of blessing the family. It is Abraham's "Priesthood," the patriarchal order of the priesthood. This priesthood blesses the families of the earth because it is the power by which the family can be eternal. Those who receive and embrace the Abrahamic covenant are blessed for time and eternity. It is the covenant through which God creates eternal families.

The "Priesthood" of Abraham shall bless "all the families of the earth" because every member of every family who ever lived will one day have his or her temple work done. That is a blessing to all the families of the earth. Performing that temple work and making those ordinances available for all is the greatest responsibility that we, as Abraham's seed, have.

*Unto thy seed will I give this land.* This is the blessing of property and inheritance. Abraham's direct posterity was promised the land of Canaan. Like the other blessings of the covenant, this blessing was repeated to

Abraham at different times in his life. In Genesis 13, the Lord reiterated this same promise of Canaan (Genesis 13:14–17).

Canaan is familiar to us as the promised land of the Old Testament. Moses led the children of Israel out of Egypt, where they had been held in captivity for centuries. Moses then led them through the wilderness for forty years. Following Moses's death, his successor, Joshua, led them across the River Jordan and into Canaan. These were Abraham's descendants, and this was their promised land.

Throughout the Book of Mormon, we see the repeated promise, "Inasmuch as ye shall keep the commandments of God ye shall prosper in the land" (Alma 36:1). This follows the same promise given to Abraham. Lehi's descendants likely understood this promise to be part of their Abrahamic covenant blessings.[35]

What greater blessings could any parent ask for? In this covenant, Abraham was promised a great family nation. They would bear the Lord's priesthood and bless all the nations of the earth. And they would have an inheritance to live in forever.

Just as homesteads have been passed from generation to generation in mortality, the blessing of Canaan (the celestial kingdom) is passed through Abraham's seed, specifically the tribes of Israel. In showing Ezekiel the blessings that flow from the temple, the Lord's angel also took the occasion to teach firsthand this blessing of Canaan. "Thus saith the Lord God; This shall be the border, whereby ye shall inherit the land according to the twelve tribes of Israel: Joseph shall have two portions" (Ezekiel 47:13). The land that we hope to inherit is the celestial kingdom. That land is passed to Abraham's descendants through the twelve tribes of Israel, with Joseph being given a double portion.

Abraham was also given great personal blessings. The Lord promised Him that He would bless those who blessed Abraham and curse those who cursed him. This is a constant reminder that the Lord is ever mindful of His covenant children. It is likewise a reminder that those who embrace Abraham's covenant will be blessed, while those who reject the covenant will be rejected of the Lord and excluded from its blessings.

## The Sanctuary of the Covenant

Abraham received these promises through a temple-like experience. We earlier learned that biblical covenants were received in a sanctuary. For our purposes, we can substitute the word *sanctuary* with *temple*. In every temple is an altar, which itself expresses the symbolism of a temple on a smaller scale. When Abraham received these promises, he promptly built "an altar unto the Lord, who appeared unto him" (Genesis 12:7). This is the first and most explicit indication we receive that the covenant promises made to Abraham were made in a sacred place.

The next verse emphasizes this: "And he removed from thence unto a mountain [a scriptural symbol of the temple] on the east of Beth-el [literally "house of God"], and pitched his tent, having Beth-el on the west, and Hai on the east: and there he builded an altar unto the Lord, and called upon the name of the Lord" (Genesis 12:8). Notably, Abraham returned to this place frequently to call upon the Lord (see Genesis 13:1–4, 18).

A covenant this sacred must surely be effectuated in a sacred place. That sacred place is a temple. Like Abraham, we should return often to the place where we are promised blessings and continue to call upon the Lord.

## The Blessings to Us

Those who receive the Lord's gospel are called Abraham's seed. This is the great blessing that we as Latter-day Saints must recognize and treasure. We are both the fulfillment and the heirs of the blessings promised to Abraham.

What roles do these same blessings have in our lives? That answer is found in large part in Doctrine and Covenants 132, where the promises made to Abraham are repeated in the latter days. This section of the scriptures gives the fulfillment of the promises made to one of Abraham's seed, Joseph Smith. At the same time, it teaches that those same promises belong to Abraham's seed, namely you and me.

*I will make of thee a great nation.* This is the blessing of eternal families and eternal lives. This becomes clearer in subsequent promises where Abraham's seed is compared to the stars in the heavens and the sand on the sea shore (Genesis 15:5; 22:17). As part of this same covenant, the Lord promised to Joseph Smith "crowns of eternal lives in the eternal worlds" (D&C 132:55).

What are eternal lives? To any and all who enter into the new and everlasting covenant of marriage and are sealed by the Holy Spirit of Promise, the Lord promises "a continuation of the seeds forever and ever" (D&C 132:19). This is the modern-day revelation equivalent of the words in Abraham's promise. Through the sealing power restored by Elijah to Joseph Smith found only in the temple, the blessings of the fathers are again ours.

This is the blessing of eternal families. As discussed in the previous chapter, "In order to attain to the highest degree of the celestial kingdom, every person must find his place in the celestial family organization."[36] This "celestial family organization" is the blessing promised to us of eternal families.

This blessing certainly applies to mortality as well, as a celestial marriage on earth gives rise to a celestial family on earth and in heaven.

*They shall bear this ministry and Priesthood unto all nations.* The priesthood is the power and authority to act in the name of God, and it has been restored. This priesthood is, first and foremost, a responsibility. "We who live in this day are those whom God appointed before birth to be his priesthood representations on the earth in this dispensation. We are the house of Israel. In our hands lie the sacred powers of bringing to pass the ennobling work of being saviors on Mount Zion in the latter days."[37] On both sides of the veil, we, the descendants of Abraham—largely through Ephraim and Manasseh, carry this priesthood for the purpose of serving the Lord and carrying His gospel to all nations.

This priesthood is also an actual dominion—it is a right to rule in righteousness, just as a king or queen has a right to rule over his or her kingdom. The blessings of the priesthood are endless. In a specific reference to Abraham, the Lord pronounced to the Prophet Joseph Smith, "I seal upon you your exaltation, and prepare a throne for you in the kingdom of my Father, with Abraham your father" (D&C 132:49). The throne in the kingdom of the Father promised to Joseph is a reference to eternal priesthood power and the right to rule and reign forever, with Abraham, his son Isaac, and his grandson Jacob.

If we are worthy, this throne of priesthood is ours, on earth and throughout the eternities. This priesthood is a dominion; it is the authority to act in the name of the King, and even to become a king and priest, a queen and priestess. It is the right to rule in the eternities. "Those who receive this highest reward may become eventually kings and queens, priests and priestesses unto the Most High, and are called gods, even the sons of God."[38] The blessing of the priesthood, promised to Abraham, is the blessing of eventually becoming kings and queens, priests and priestesses.

This is the same blessing of the patriarchal order discussed in the previous chapter. It is inseparably connected with the blessing of eternal families and eternal reign.

The patriarchal priesthood is at the center of these three blessings of the Abrahamic covenant, perhaps for a good reason. It is both the power through which these blessings are administered and received as well as the blessing itself.

This blessing pertains both to mortality and to eternity. Holding the priesthood in mortality is an honor that relatively few have enjoyed throughout the earth's history. The same can be said for receiving the ordinances of the priesthood. Those who have received those blessings in mortality are charged with the tremendous responsibility of making those same blessings available to others through both missionary and temple work. Abraham's seed in mortality are those who have received those blessings and must pass them on.

*Unto thy seed will I give this land.* This is the blessing of the celestial kingdom. Canaan, the promised land, is an unmistakable scriptural type of the celestial kingdom. Canaan was the land prepared for Abraham and the Israelites anciently. The throne prepared for Joseph and Abraham belongs to the eternal Canaan, the celestial kingdom (D&C 132:49).

A throne in the same kingdom and principality awaits Abraham's other children through the covenant named after him.

This blessing certainly has an earthly application, as the land of Canaan is no doubt the most coveted and fought over real estate in earth's history. However, this blessing primarily refers to the celestial kingdom and the eternities. The war for that kingdom isn't be won with the blood of soldiers or civilians; it has been won through the blood of the Savior. And it will be won for those who make and keep sacred temple covenants, as that is how we put into practice the Savior's Atonement.

## The Blessings of Endless Posterity, Endless Priesthood, and Celestial Inheritance

These three main blessings are often grouped together, as they were to Abraham, because they are inseparable. Referencing all of the blessings of the Abrahamic covenant, President George Q. Cannon, a member of the First Presidency in the late nineteenth century, taught,

> God has . . . promised us that we shall sit upon thrones, that we shall have crowns, and that we shall have a posterity as numerous as the stars in heaven, as countless as the sand upon the sea shore; for, said He, "I seal upon you the blessings of kingdoms, or thrones, of principalities, of powers, and of dominions. I seal upon you the blessings of Abraham, of Isaac, and of Jacob. I seal upon you the promise that you shall come forth in the morning of the first resurrection clothed with glory, immortality and eternal lives." These are the promises that are made to the Latter-day Saints. . . . The Lord promised to Abraham that as the stars of heaven were innumerable in multitude, and as the sand on the sea shore was countless, so his seed should be. That same promise has been sealed upon your heads, ye Latter-day Saints who have been faithful.[39]

## The Blessings Sought and the Blessings Promised

When Abraham listed the blessings he was seeking, he did not specifically name some of the blessings that he was ultimately promised. His prayers for posterity and priesthood were specifically answered, but he did not pray to be given Canaan or any other land. He prayed for greater peace, happiness, and rest. He prayed for instructions. He prayed to be a prince of peace and a father of many nations. He prayed for greater understanding and to be a greater follower of righteousness. The Lord, in His infinite goodness and wisdom, chose to answer these prayers with the blessings of the patriarchal order—the promises of posterity, priesthood, and promised land.

We must recognize that the blessings of the temple *are* the blessings of greater happiness, peace, and rest. The blessings of becoming a prince of peace are found in the temple. The blessings of greater learning, understanding, and righteousness are found in the ordinances and covenants of the temple.

Too often we don't immediately recognize the blessings the Lord bestows upon us because they aren't in the form we requested. If we find ourselves frustrated because life seems to not be what we envisioned—even when we have entered into covenant and have been faithful to it—we have the assurance of the Savior that the promised blessings will arrive.

> Ask, and it shall be given you; seek, and ye shall find; knock, and it shall be opened unto you: for every one that asketh receiveth; and he that seeketh findeth; and to him that knocketh it shall be opened. Or what man is there of you, whom if his son ask bread, will he give him a stone? Or if he ask a fish, will he give him a serpent? If ye then, being evil, know how to give good gifts unto your children, how much more shall your Father which is in heaven give good things to them that ask him? (Matthew 7:7–11)

Abraham's experiences in these first two chapters are the first of several examples when he and Sarah did not at first receive the exact blessings they sought. Beginning here, their story is a great lesson to us of how our Father in Heaven blesses us. He rarely gives us the precise blessings that we perceive we need at the exact moment we want them. But, in the end, His word is always sure. The faith and patience exercised by Abraham and Sarah offer marvelous insights for us to travel this journey toward the promised covenant blessings.

- *Abraham's journey began by seeking the specific blessings promised to the fathers. In response to Abraham's quest, the Lord promised him great blessings.*

- *Those blessings fit into three main categories: posterity, priesthood, and the land of promise—the same inseparable blessings promised to us through the Abrahamic covenant.*
- *The blessing of posterity is ours through the blessing of eternal lives, as taught in the Doctrine and Covenants. This is the blessing of eternal families. As eternal families begin on earth, this is a blessing to be received in mortality and eternity.*
- *The blessing of priesthood is ours on earth as holders of the priesthood, with many sacred obligations. This blessing is to be enjoyed in mortality and in eternity. Those of Abraham's seed who receive this blessing in mortality are under sacred obligation to help others receive it through missionary and temple work. Both the Genesis and the Abraham accounts promise this blessing of the priesthood specifically to all the families of the earth. The blessing of priesthood is also ours for the eternities, as we may become kings and queens or priests and priestesses to God in the eternities.*
- *The blessing of the promised land, symbolized by the land of Canaan, represents an inheritance in the celestial kingdom.*

# *Genesis 14*

## *Abraham's Encounter with Melchizedek*

**A*mong the blessings*** Abraham sought and received were to be "a prince of peace" and a "High Priest" (Abraham 1:2). In Genesis 14, Abraham had a cherished meeting with a prophet who held both of these titles: Melchizedek. Like Abraham's experiences in Genesis 12 and 13, where the Lord promised Abraham great blessings, Genesis 14 is a temple experience for Abraham, because he received an actual ordination, or ordinance of the patriarchal order. Melchizedek had the blessings that Abraham was seeking, and Melchizedek held the priesthood keys to share these blessings with Abraham.

### *A Great High Priest*

The Bible says little about Melchizedek. Aside from a few verses in Genesis 14 and another verse in Psalm 110, the Old Testament offers nothing about this great patriarch. The Apostle Paul gave a little more information in Hebrews 5 and 7, but that is still not a lot. On the other hand, Melchizedek appears much more prominently in modern revelation. The Joseph Smith Translation of Genesis 14 gives us several key verses that don't appear in the standard King James edition. Likewise, Alma 13 and several sections in the Doctrine and Covenants are quite helpful.

Genesis 14:18 introduces Melchizedek as "the priest of the most high God." Alma 13:14 likewise names Melchizedek as a "high priest," just as Abraham sought to become. Doctrine and Covenants 107 echoes this title and takes it even further. Not only was Melchizedek a high priest, he "was such a great high priest" that the greater priesthood, formerly called "the Holy Priesthood, after the Order of the Son of God," was named after Melchizedek (D&C 107:2–3). Abraham's encounter with Melchizedek in Genesis 14 was no coincidence. Abraham was in search of the promised blessings, and Melchizedek was the high priest who held the keys to those blessings.

What is a high priest? Why did Abraham have to go to Melchizedek as part of his quest for these blessings?

## A High Priest in the Patriarchal Order

The LDS Bible Dictionary gives insight on this point. It lists two definitions of a high priest (see Bible Dictionary, "High priest"). According to the first definition, a high priest is an office in the Melchizedek Priesthood to which Adam and all the ancient patriarchs belonged. In this sense, a high priest is one who belongs to the patriarchal order that Abraham sought (see Alma 13:1–3, 6–9, 11). From this, we learn that a high priest is a priest who has entered the order of the Son of God, or the patriarchal order of the priesthood.

This is why Abraham sought out Melchizedek as part of his quest for blessings. Even though Genesis 12 and 13 were revelatory temple experiences for Abraham, there is no indication that Abraham was actually physically ordained or received the necessary ordinances in those chapters. Like anyone even in our day, Abraham would have had to seek out a priesthood holder with keys to receive a priesthood ordinance or ordination. That is how priesthood keys operate. Melchizedek was a high priest of this order, and he held the keys to bestow the blessings that Abraham sought.

## A High Priest under the Law of Moses

The second definition in the Bible Dictionary gives further insight into the role of a high priest. "Under the law of Moses the presiding officer of the Aaronic Priesthood was called the high priest. The office was hereditary [meaning patriarchal] and came through the firstborn among the family of Aaron, Aaron himself being the first high priest of the Aaronic order" (Bible Dictionary, "High priest"). Therefore, a high priest, in the biblical sense, encompasses both the Aaronic and Melchizedek Priesthoods.

The functions performed by Aaron and the other high priests under the Mosaic law sheds further light on the blessings sought by Abraham. On the day of Atonement—the most holy day of the year—the high priest, clothed in white linen, offered sacrifices in the temple. One of these offerings was a bullock, which was meant to symbolize atonement for sins. The other offering was a ram, like the one found by Abraham and Isaac in the thicket on Mount Moriah in Genesis 22. As the Lord commanded Abraham to sacrifice Isaac, this ram was offered as a burnt offering that was to be completely consumed by fire, with smoke ascending to heaven like a prayer. These offerings were on behalf of the high priest and his house. The high priest was to also offer another ram and two male goats on behalf of the entire house of Israel. One of these goats was to be driven away with the sins of Israel symbolically cast on it (see Bible Dictionary, "Fasts"). This is where the modern term of a "scapegoat" comes from.

After making the sacrifice of these animals, the high priest then did something remarkable that could only be done one day a year and that he alone could do. He entered the Holy of Holies—the symbolic presence of God. There, the high priest took live coals from the altar, together with incense, and "applied" the blood of the sin offerings to make a symbolic atonement, just as we plead to the Father to "apply the atoning blood of Christ that we may receive forgiveness of our sins" (Mosiah 4:2). He does this symbolically, first on behalf of himself and his family, and then for the house of Israel (see Bible Dictionary, "Fasts").

The symbolic lessons in the high priest's actions are overwhelming. First, the high priest served as the one chosen among a multitude to bring the blessings of the Atonement to his house, and then to all of Israel. It may be in this sense that Abraham sought to "administer" the blessings of the patriarchal order (Abraham 1:2). The children of Israel depended on the high priest; his ability to make this symbolic intercession for them was a symbolic matter of life and death.

Second, the high priest was counted as one who was worthy to stand in the presence of God. Entering the Holy of Holies was the sole privilege of the high priest anciently. Through the fulness of the priesthood, entering the presence of God is also the privilege of all the "priests of the Most High, after the order of Melchizedek" (D&C 76:57). Through this order of the priesthood, many, many more will be blessed to "come unto Mount Zion, and unto the city of the living God, the heavenly place, the holiest of all" (D&C 76:66).

Here are two important functions of the high priest of the Mosaic law that prefigured the blessings of the Abrahamic covenant. First, the high priest offered intercession for his people through sacrifices that represented the Atonement. This was a fulfillment of the promise that Abraham's seed would be the means of blessing all the families of the earth (see Abraham 2:11). Second, the high priest entered the symbolic presence of God on the day of Atonement. This prefigured the inheritance of the celestial kingdom promised to Abraham and his seed (see Genesis 13:15).

## Who Is a High Priest?

With the help of these insights, let's answer the question of who is a high priest. A high priest is one who finds his divine right and place in the patriarchal order. He does so by great works of faith and righteousness. A high priest is also one who serves. He puts the Atonement into full practice in his own life and makes its blessings available to his people. He is the one worthy to enter the presence of God. He does so by virtue of all vows or all covenants.

Abraham wanted to be a high priest. He wanted to be able to serve his people just as the high priest served in the temple. He wanted to be able to enter the presence of God and help others do the same, including, most prominently, his own family.

## Abraham's Temple Experience with Melchizedek

Understanding Melchizedek's role as a high priest means we can understand more of his experience with Abraham. This experience begins after Abraham had defeated multiple enemies in an epic battle. In addition to Abraham's great accomplishments as an astronomer, missionary, teacher, and shepherd, he was also a celebrated war hero. After rescuing his nephew and defeating armies, Abraham returned home and was confronted by the king of Sodom (yes, that Sodom) and others, whose armies he had just defeated. That encounter is actually quite important, as we will discuss, and it is here that Melchizedek appeared, as if from nowhere.

As Melchizedek appeared, he "brought forth bread and wine" (Genesis 14:18). The Joseph Smith Translation expounds on this, revealing that he "brake bread and blest it; and he blest the wine, he being the priest of the most high God" (JST Genesis 14:17). This reference to the ordinance of the sacrament gives us the first indication that Abraham's experience was indeed a temple experience. While we now administer this ordinance in chapels, every Old Testament reference to the sacrament takes place inside the temple. In the tabernacle and ancient temple, twelve loaves of bread (shewbread, more precisely) were spread out every Sabbath, representing the twelve tribes of Israel (Leviticus 24:5–9; Exodus 25:23–30; 29:33–34). The temple workers partook of this bread as the sacrament. "The most impressive rite of the temple was the 'drinking of the new wine by the entire assembly,' which was to symbolize a ransom or redemption."[40]

There's no other reference in the Old Testament to the sacramental bread and wine being administered outside of the temple. At the outset, it is clear that Abraham's meeting with Melchizedek was something holy.

Now back to the king of Sodom, who rudely interrupted Abraham's meeting with Melchizedek. Talk about enmity and contrast—here was the prophet Abraham meeting with the great High Priest Melchizedek. They came face to face with the king of Sodom, a place so wicked that it would soon be destroyed. This is a most curious confrontation between the Lord's messengers and the king of Satan's greatest stronghold on earth.

What business did they have together? Well, Abraham obviously had serious spiritual business to conduct with Melchizedek. He wanted Melchizedek to teach him and bless him, but the king of Sodom wanted to interrupt this divine teaching opportunity. The king of Sodom approached Abraham, trying to strike a deal over the spoils that Abraham had won in his military victory to free Lot. The king of Sodom essentially proposed buying people from Abraham: "Give me the persons, and take the goods to thyself" (Genesis 14:21).

Abraham, however, wanted absolutely nothing to do with this proposal, having previously made a covenant with the Lord to take nothing from the king of Sodom. "I have lift up mine hand unto the Lord, the most high God, the possessor of heaven and earth, that I will not take from a thread even to a shoelatchet, and that I will not take any thing that is thine, lest thou shouldest say, I have made Abram rich" (Genesis 14:22–23).

Abraham then sent the king of Sodom on his way, unwilling to sell out his covenant for the goods of the world offered by the king. Oh, that we could all be so true to our covenants, that we all could all avoid buying anything from or selling anything to the modern kings of Sodom and stick to our business with the modern Melchizedeks.

Free from the king of Sodom, Abraham and Melchizedek could continue their sacred experience together. Where the King James Version ends, the Joseph Smith Translation picks up. This scripture is magnificent in the scope of the blessings of the priesthood it describes.

> And Melchizedek lifted up his voice and blessed Abram.
>
> Now Melchizedek was a man of faith, who wrought righteousness; and when a child he feared God, and stopped the mouths of lions, and quenched the violence of fire.
>
> And thus, having been approved of God, he was ordained an high priest after the order of the covenant which God made with Enoch,
>
> It being after the order of the Son of God; which order came, not by man, nor the will of man; neither by father nor mother; neither by beginning of days nor end of years; but of God;
>
> And it was delivered unto men by the calling of his own voice, according to his own will, unto as many as believed on his name.
>
> For God having sworn unto Enoch and unto his seed with an oath by himself; that every one being ordained after this order and calling

> should have power, by faith, to break mountains, to divide the seas, to dry up waters, to turn them out of their course;
>
> To put at defiance the armies of nations, to divide the earth, to break every band, to stand in the presence of God; to do all things according to his will, according to his command, subdue principalities and powers; and this by the will of the Son of God which was from before the foundation of the world.
>
> And men having this faith, coming up unto this order of God, were translated and taken up into heaven.
>
> And now, Melchizedek was a priest of this order; therefore he obtained peace in Salem, and was called the Prince of peace.
>
> And his people wrought righteousness, and obtained heaven, and sought for the city of Enoch which God had before taken, separating it from the earth, having reserved it unto the latter days, or the end of the world;
>
> And hath said, and sworn with an oath, that the heavens and the earth should come together; and the sons of God should be tried so as by fire.
>
> And this Melchizedek, having thus established righteousness, was called the king of heaven by his people, or, in other words, the King of peace.
>
> And he lifted up his voice, and he blessed Abram, being the high priest, and the keeper of the storehouse of God;
>
> Him whom God had appointed to receive tithes for the poor.
>
> Wherefore, Abram paid unto him tithes of all that he had, of all the riches which he possessed, which God had given him more than that which he had need.
>
> And it came to pass, that God blessed Abram, and gave unto him riches, and honor, and lands for an everlasting possession; according to the covenant which he had made, and according to the blessing wherewith Melchizedek had blessed him. (JST Genesis 14:25–40)

From the Joseph Smith Translation, we learn much more about Melchizedek than we would otherwise know. We learn of his righteous works and his faith exercised since childhood. We see why Abraham sought out Melchizedek, as he held the keys to the blessings Abraham was seeking. By now, no one should be surprised to see still more references to the patriarchal order of the priesthood—the blessings of the temple. There are no fewer than six such references in this block of scripture.

This scripture teaches of Enoch, by no coincidence. The blessings of this order of the priesthood also include the blessings of Enoch, which we commonly know as the blessings of Zion. This scripture also provides a glimpse into the association of Enoch, Melchizedek, and Abraham. Melchizedek is likened to Enoch, and Enoch appears throughout ancient writings as a personal exemplar and role model for Abraham. In fact, the whole premise of E. Douglas Clark's *magnum opus*—the most comprehensive LDS study of Abraham ever written—is that Abraham sought to emulate Enoch's Zion.[41] On that note, we can safely conclude that one of the purposes of the patriarchal order of the priesthood and its accompanying temple ordinances is to build up Zion, just as Enoch did.

The blessings of this order of the priesthood also include the power to perform miracles, or more specifically "to break mountains, to divide the seas, to dry up waters, to turn them out of their course" (JST Genesis 14:30). These are clear references to the priesthood, the power of God to defy natural laws and work miracles. Only a righteous and faithful holder of this priesthood—a priest—can work such miracles. Therefore, these blessings may be called the blessings of a priest or a priestess.

Further, the blessings include the power to "put at defiance the armies of nations, to divide the earth, to break every band" and "subdue principalities and powers" (JST Genesis 14:31). These blessings also pertain to the priesthood and its power of government and dominion. These are the familiar rights of a governmental ruler—a king or a queen.

Finally, these blessings include being called a prince of peace and standing in the presence of God (JST Genesis 14:31, 34). These are the blessings of priesthood power that we should all seek. They enable us to stand in the presence of God, like the high priest in the ancient temple on the day of Atonement, in accordance with the purpose of the temple endowment, as described by Brigham Young.

This scripture does not just list the great blessings and priesthood power held by Melchizedek and sought by Abraham. This scripture also describes the blessings *bestowed* by Melchizedek to Abraham. The blessings given to Abraham by the hand of Melchizedek were none other than the temple endowment.[42]

Joseph Smith taught, "Abraham says to Melchizedek, I believe all that thou hast taught me concerning the priesthood and the coming of the Son of Man; so Melchizedek ordained Abraham and sent him away. Abraham rejoiced, saying, Now I have a priesthood."[43]

What priesthood and ordination did Abraham receive from Melchizedek? The obvious answer in reading the Joseph Smith Translation of Genesis 14 is the patriarchal order of the priesthood. As taught by latter-day prophets, this priesthood is only received in the temple of the Lord.

## What Abraham's Experience with Melchizedek Means to Us

The blessings from Abraham's experience with Melchizedek are the same blessings promised to us through the temple. The blessings of becoming a king and a high priest or a queen and priestess are available to us through the ordinances of the temple.

- *After receiving the promises of endless posterity, priesthood, and a land of inheritance, Abraham met with Melchizedek.*
- *Melchizedek was the high priest who held the priesthood keys to bestow the blessings of the patriarchal priesthood that Abraham had been seeking.*
- *Even though Abraham had received a promise of those blessings, he had not yet received them. To receive these blessings, Abraham sought the blessing of becoming a high priest.*
- *In the Old Testament, a high priest is described in two different ways: a patriarch who had entered into the patriarchal order and received the higher blessings of the priesthood or the presiding Aaronic Priesthood holder in the ancient temple.*
- *The high priest in the ancient temple performed sacred functions that teach us what it means to hold this calling and title. The high priest offered sacrifices on the day of Atonement on behalf of himself and his family, and then on behalf of the house of Israel, meaning all who are a part of the Abrahamic covenant. On the day of Atonement, the most sacred day of the year, the high priest entered the Holy of Holies—the*

*symbolic presence of God—and applied the blood of the sacrifice to make atonement for the sins of all of Israel.*

- *Abraham's meeting with Melchizedek began with Melchizedek administering the emblems of the sacrament. The Old Testament only records this ordinance being administered in the temple.*
- *Melchizedek blessed Abraham according to the blessings previously promised from the Lord: the promise of Zion, the power to perform miracles by the priesthood, governmental rule by the priesthood, and the power to become a prince of peace and stand in the presence of God, like the ancient high priest in the Holy of Holies.*
- *Melchizedek gave Abraham the ordinances of the temple, meaning the blessings of the patriarchal order of the priesthood.*
- *These same blessings are available to us today through the ordinances of the temple.*

# Genesis 15

## "Look Now toward Heaven, and Tell the Stars"

**Abraham and Sarah** still awaited the posterity promised in Genesis 12. They remained childless after more than a decade since then. In Genesis 15, Abraham had another temple experience, wherein the Lord reiterated the promised blessings of the covenant. This time, however, there is a notable difference in one of those promises.

### The Blessings to Abraham

"And [the Lord] brought [Abraham] forth abroad, and said, Look now toward heaven, and tell the stars, if thou be able to number them: and [the Lord] said unto [Abraham], So shall thy seed be. And he believed in the Lord; and he counted it to him for righteousness" (Genesis 15:5–6).

When the Lord first promised Abraham posterity, the promise was simply that Abraham would be a great nation (Genesis 12:2; Abraham 2:9). Later, the Lord expanded that promise by comparing Abraham's seed to the dust of the earth (Genesis 13:16). That same promise was later given by comparing Abraham's posterity to the sand upon the seashore (Genesis 22:17). That promise alone is rather infinite, as it would be impossible to count either the particles of dust on the dry places of the earth or the grains of sand on the watery seashore.

Here, however, the promise takes the metaphor of the stars in the heavens. What is different about the stars in the heavens? Are they any more innumerable than dust particles or sand grains? The difference is not so much in number. All the comparisons are beyond the ability of humans to count.

No, the difference in this blessing lies in where the blessing of posterity is found. The stars are found in the heavens, or in the eternities. Dust and sand are found on the earth. The blessings now promised to Abraham as he grows in faith and good works are to be found in the eternities.

This point becomes clear, as the Lord taught to Joseph Smith and to us. "Abraham received promises concerning his seed, and of the fruit of his loins—from whose loins ye[44] are, namely, my servant Joseph—which were to continue so long as they were in the world; and as touching Abraham and his seed, out of the world they should continue; both in the world and out of the world should they continue as innumerable as the stars; or, if ye were to count the sand upon the seashore ye could not number them" (D&C 132:30). In other words, the blessing of posterity promised to Abraham (and to us) were now specifically to overflow this world and into the eternities.

The Joseph Smith Translation of this same chapter sheds further light on the growing and eternal scope of the promises made to Abraham. With respect to the promise of Canaan, Abraham inquired of the Lord, and the Lord answered.

> And Abram said, Lord God, how wilt thou give me this land for an everlasting inheritance?
>
> And the Lord said, Though thou wast dead, yet am I not able to give it thee?
>
> And if thou shalt die, yet thou shalt possess it, for the day cometh, that the Son of Man shall live; but how can he live if he be not dead? he must first be quickened.
>
> And it came to pass, that Abram looked forth and saw the days of the Son of Man, and was glad, and his soul found rest, and he believed

> in the Lord; and the Lord counted it unto him for righteousness. (JST Genesis 15:9–12)

The blessings promised to Abraham in this temple experience were to be found in the resurrection and in the eternities. In the sand on the seashore and in the dust of Canaan, we see time. In the stars up in the heavens and in the celestial Canaan, we see eternity.

## The Sanctuary of the Covenant

Genesis 15 was also a temple experience for Abraham. The chapter doesn't specifically mention an altar, as in Genesis 12 and 13, but such is implied for two reasons. First, the Lord was speaking to Abraham. Any such occasion constitutes a temple experience, broadly speaking. Second, the Lord commanded Abraham to offer up sacrifices (Genesis 15:9). Sacrifices are offered on altars. Just as before, a sacred interaction with the Lord necessarily occurs in a sacred space: a temple.

Genesis 15 leaves no doubt that the blessings of posterity, priesthood, and the promised land are eternal blessings. They are so innumerable that they flood over the banks of time and fill eternity.

## A Message of Hope to the Childless

Through His prophets, the Lord has sought to comfort those who have not been blessed with a righteous marriage companion through no fault or choice of their own. President Harold B. Lee taught, "You . . . who have not yet accepted a proposal of marriage, if you make yourselves worthy and ready to go to the house of the Lord and have faith in this sacred principle of celestial marriage for eternity, even though the privilege of marriage does not come to you now in mortality, the Lord will reward you in due time and no blessing will be denied you."[45]

Quoting another latter-day prophet, Brigham Young, President Lee also taught, "There are . . . who have not as yet had an acceptable offer of marriage or if married have not been able to have children. . . . To these President [Brigham] Young made a promise for which the plan of salvation provides the fulfillment. He said, 'Many of the sisters grieve because they are not blessed with offspring. You will see the time when you will have millions of children around you. If you are faithful to your covenants, you will be mothers of nations.'"[46] These blessings certainly apply to men and women alike, married and unmarried.

These are wonderful promises, no doubt. They are clearly the blessings promised to Abraham, and they fit beautifully within the Genesis 15 message. If posterity on earth escapes a righteous person, he or she can "look now toward heaven" and envision posterity like the stars (Genesis 15:5).

Sarah should serve as a beacon of hope for all who look toward heaven for the fulfillment of the Abrahamic blessings they seek. Genesis 18:11 teaches that Sarah had already entered menopause, yet she gave birth to Isaac three chapters and many years later. She was at least ninety when she gave birth to Isaac. With this timetable, there is no earthly explanation for Isaac's birth. By all mortal measures, Sarah shouldn't have been able to have posterity.

Still, the Lord fulfilled the promise.

For many, the Isaac experience might not come in mortality. The ninetieth year, when Sarah finally received her blessing of parenthood, might arrive in the next life for some. The elusive blessing of parenthood might come only then, beyond the explanation and understanding of mortality. But it has been promised. If you are faithful, it will come.

The endowment also presents a great reassurance of the blessings of heaven. Unlike the marriage covenant or the blessings of posterity on earth, the endowment is completely within the agency and reach of everyone. Some may not be able to receive the ordinance of celestial marriage in this life—through no choice of their own—but they can most definitely receive the blessings of the endowment if they are worthy.

When you qualify for a temple recommend and receive the blessings of the endowment, listen carefully and watch closely. Through the whisperings and insights of the Holy Ghost, you will find many promises and blessings clearly pertaining to the highest blessings of the priesthood within the endowment itself. In fact, those promises and blessings are to be found throughout all of the endowment. Those promises are the Lord's assurance that no blessing will be withheld from you if you remain faithful to the endowment.

To those men and women without children, as you "look now toward heaven" in anticipation of the blessings awaiting you, take every step and make every effort to receive the endowment. The blessings of the endowment are essential to the eternity you seek. They will strengthen your faith and hope for receiving the remaining blessings of the Abrahamic covenant in heaven, if not on earth—in the eternities, if not in mortality.

## A Personal Experience in Looking Now toward Heaven

Maybe my own experience on this subject can illustrate the point. When I was sixteen, a truly inspired patriarch placed his hands on my head and pronounced a beautiful blessing on me through the priesthood he held. The Spirit was overwhelming. I still get goosebumps just thinking about it. There was no question this blessing came straight from the Lord through His ordained patriarch. In fact, the blessings of the Abrahamic covenant are, in a real sense, a patriarchal blessing to all of us through Father Abraham.

Among the specific blessings pronounced on me was that I would marry a choice companion and love her with all of my heart, and she would return this love in a similar manner. We would be blessed with beautiful sons and daughters. I didn't care what else was promised in that blessing. Anything else was all gravy, as far as I was concerned (and still am concerned to this day). All I wanted out of life was a wife who would love me. She and I would live happily ever after with our sons and daughters. Nothing else in life would truly matter.

On August 18, 1992, in the Manti Utah Temple, my dream came true, and the blessing was fulfilled. We have lived quite happily in love since.

Another part of the blessing also became reality when our first daughter, Heidi, was born. She was absolutely beautiful and perfect, just as foretold in my patriarchal blessing. Then we were blessed with

Kayla. Then came Claire, Anna, and Robyn. They were all wonderful, intelligent children, just as promised years before. Without question, they are among the most valiant and choice spirits of Heavenly Father. I love them all and would gladly give the world for any of them.

But the day that we had the ultrasound for Robyn opened one of the most difficult periods of my life. Cami and I weren't getting any younger. Cami had difficult pregnancies, and three of our babies were born premature. They weren't easy babies by any means, and the year or two surrounding each pregnancy and birth were as taxing on Cami and me as they were rewarding. We knew we couldn't physically keep having children. And the ultrasound showed . . . a girl. She's an adorable, awesome girl, and we've loved every day of her life. But she's not a boy, not an Isaac.

I felt horribly ungrateful over my lack of an Isaac. I was blessed with a beautiful family. I should have been grateful for such a blessing. I had four—going on five—healthy, beautiful, lively daughters and a wonderful spouse who loved me back. Instead of being grateful for these blessings, I dwelled on the blessing I didn't have, and that tore at me. I was embarrassed at my lack of gratitude.

Probably the strongest emotion I felt was disappointment in myself. I wondered constantly what I had done to disqualify myself from the blessing of a son, promised to me in my patriarchal blessing. I'm sure many childless and single people torment themselves with the same question. What had I done to lose my Isaac? The thought gnawed on me day and night for longer than I care to admit.

Well-meaning and sincere people could see how much I wanted a son. They would tell me, "You'll have sons-in-law and grandsons one day." Thanks, but that didn't help. It even made me grit my teeth. Sometimes it even tempted me to slug someone (not seriously tempted, though). Still, their well-intentioned counsel didn't help. Maybe some childless people feel the same way when other good-hearted people try to offer words of comfort. I learned for myself that those well wishes don't mean that much when it comes to a subject like being single or childless, even though I was neither. Such subjects are just too personal for easy consolation.

In all of my doubt and self-blaming—which I'm sure Abraham and Sarah endured on a much larger scale—I did find some doctrine that offered me comfort and hope. I read the words of an Apostle—a prophet, seer, and revelator. Elder John A. Widtsoe said,

> It should always be kept in mind that the realization of the promises made [in a patriarchal blessing] may come in this or the future life. Men have stumbled at times because promised blessings have not occurred in this life. They have failed to remember that, in the gospel, life with all its activities continues forever and that the labors of earth may be continued in heaven. Besides, the Giver of the blessings, the Lord, reserves the right to have them become active in our lives, as suits His divine purpose. We and our blessings are in the hands of the Lord. But, there is the general testimony that when the gospel law has been obeyed, the promised blessings have been realized.[47]

To this, President Harold B. Lee added,

> [A] patriarch of [a] stake spoke at [a] funeral . . . [and] said, "When a patriarch pronounces an inspired blessing, such a blessing encompasses the whole of life, not just this phase we call mortality."
>
> "If in this life only we have hope in Christ, we are of all men most miserable," said the Apostle Paul. If we fail to understand this great truth, we will be miserable in time of need, and then sometimes our faith may be challenged. But if we have a faith that looks beyond the grave and trusts in divine Providence to bring all things in their proper perspective in due time, then we have hope, and our fears are calmed . . . Life does not end with mortal death.[48]

And with that reassurance, I learned the blessing of an eternal perspective. Such is the lesson of looking up toward heaven, as the Lord taught Abraham. Some blessings are stars, not dust or sand. They are to be received in the eternities, not necessarily in mortality. In fact, most of our blessings depend on our enduring to the end and being fulfilled in eternity, not in time.

Said poet Rossiter Raymond, "Life is eternal; and love is immortal; and death is only a horizon; and a horizon is nothing save the limit of our sight."[49] Like Abraham and Sarah, we sometimes have to look beyond the earthly horizon for fulfillment of the Lord's promises. We have to find a way to see beyond the limit of sight and into the eternities, where the choicest blessings are to be found. Staring down at the dust or the sand only frustrates and causes us to lose focus and faith when we should be looking toward heaven instead. There, the grains of sand become brilliant stars.

- *In Genesis 15, decades after Abraham and Sarah were first promised posterity as numerous as the dust of the earth and the sand of the seashore, the Lord promised Abraham posterity as innumerable as the stars in the heavens.*
- *The Lord asked Abraham to look up toward heaven to envision the blessings of his promised posterity.*
- *The simile of posterity as innumerable as the stars in the heavens may be a lesson that some blessings of the Abrahamic covenant are to be had in the eternities rather than in mortality.*
- *This lesson of heavenly posterity should be a great comfort to those who do not receive the sealing ordinance or have children in mortality.*
- *The blessings of the Abrahamic covenant are not bestowed in the sealing ordinance alone. The blessings of the endowment provide great hope, as the endowment is available to every adult who is worthy to enter the temple.*
- *The blessings of the Abrahamic covenant, as may be promised in patriarchal blessings, may be received in the eternities, not in mortality. That does not render the promises any less valid or the blessings any less real.*

# Genesis 16

## Hagar, Ishmael, and a Lesson on Celestial Marriage

**S*till childless long*** after the promises of posterity first made to Abraham in Genesis 12, and then reiterated in following chapters, Sarah gave her handmaid Hagar to Abraham so that he might become a father. This custom may seem strange and contrary to the laws of righteousness, but the Lord confirmed that Sarah's act was in accordance with the law of the time (see Doctrine and Covenants 132:34). Biblical scholars confirmed this modern-day revelation, noting that an infertile wife was obliged to bring a second wife to her husband after ten years of barrenness.[50]

No one should judge Abraham or Sarah harshly for this act. It was proper by the customs of the time and the law of the Lord, and it could not have been easy for either one of them. And so, with Abraham's second wife, Hagar, Abraham finally became a father at age eighty-six. Hagar bore a son, Ishmael (Genesis 16:16).

To this point, Sarah had been understood as the corecipient of the promised blessings along with her husband. However, no scripture in the Bible mentioned her specifically as part of Abraham's blessings up until that point. (That would change in the next chapter. The lessons of patience abound in this story.) Abraham married Hagar, and, at least by comparison to Sarah, she immediately bore a son. Hagar apparently felt somewhat superior or resentful for this experience, as Sarah confided in her husband that she "was despised in [Hagar's] eyes" over the experience (Genesis 16:5).

Can you imagine the doubt and anguish that likely filled Sarah? After all those years, it was she who was infertile. In Old Testament times especially, the miracle of childbirth was a huge part of what defined a righteous woman. Was her infertility holding Abraham back from these great blessings promised by the Lord? She must have wondered. Now on top of that, Hagar conceived almost immediately and became Sarah's rival—and it was Sarah who gave Hagar to Abraham in the first place! For that, Sarah cried to Abraham, "My wrong be upon thee" (Genesis 16:5).

Hagar fled from the home, quite distressed and obviously feeling the weight of the situation herself. An angel found her by a spring in the wilderness and instructed her to return and submit herself to Sarah, as hard as that had to be (Genesis 16:6–9). In this exchange, the messenger of the Lord made a great promise to Hagar, a promise so great that it echoed clearly of the promises made to Abraham. "I will multiply thy seed exceedingly, that it shall not be numbered for multitude. . . . Behold, thou art with child, and shalt bear a son, and shalt call his name Ishmael; because the Lord hath heard thy affliction" (Genesis 16:10–11).

However, these divine assurances were not the fulfillment of the Abrahamic covenant. That covenant would not be carried through Ishmael. When the promise of these blessings was again reiterated to Abraham after Ishmael's birth, Abraham responded to the Lord, "O that Ishmael might live before thee" (Genesis 17:18). This plea might suggest that even Abraham believed that the divine promises were being fulfilled through Hagar and Ishmael. At least, it showed that Abraham had a great love for Ishmael, even if he understood that the child of Hagar was not to carry the great covenant blessings promised to Abraham.

The Lord quickly removed any doubt or ambiguity. "Sarah thy wife shall bear thee a son indeed; and thou shalt call his name Isaac: *and I will establish my covenant with him for an everlasting covenant, and with his seed after him*. And as for Ishmael, I have heard thee: Behold,

I have blessed him, and will make him fruitful, and will multiply him exceedingly; twelve princes shall he beget, and I will make him a great nation. *But my covenant will I establish with Isaac*, which Sarah shall bear unto thee at this set time in the next year" (Genesis 17:19–21; emphasis added).

As promised here to Abraham and in Sarah's presence later (Genesis 18:10), Sarah became a mother by a pure miracle. However, when Isaac was born, the blended family did not do well, as Ishmael mocked the young Isaac (Genesis 21:9). Sarah then confronted Abraham, demanding, "Cast out this bondwoman and her son: for the son of this bondwoman shall not be heir with my son, even with Isaac" (Genesis 21:10). Certainly this was a most difficult request for Abraham because he loved his family, and Ishmael was his firstborn son (Genesis 21:11).

But Sarah's request was granted. Abraham woke up early the next day to gather provisions for Hagar and Ishmael to send them on their way (Genesis 21:14). Other ancient texts teach that Abraham provided Hagar and Ishmael with abundant provisions, including gold and silver, and he actually accompanied them for some time to assure that they were cared for.[51]

Either way, Hagar and Ishmael were gone. There is no indication that they ever returned.

## The Blessing to Us

At first glance, this appears to be just a sad story, one that might lead us to dislike Sarah and even Abraham. However, this story is actually a lesson to us on the blessings of eternal marriage.

Here is why:

Abraham's marriage with Sarah was a celestial marriage. The repeated references to the covenant through her child and her direct role in Genesis make this clear. Such a covenant marriage is eternal and creates an eternal family unit. Abraham's marriage with Hagar was a type of civil marriage. Such a marriage doesn't carry any force in the eternities. It creates a family unit that is not eternal.

After Sarah asked Abraham to send Hagar and Ishmael away, the Lord told Abraham, "Let it not be grievous in thy sight because of the lad, and because of thy bondwoman; in all that Sarah hath said unto thee, hearken unto her voice; for in Isaac shall thy seed be called" (Genesis 21:12).

This is not just a lesson for husbands to listen to their wives "in all" that they say. There was a greater plan and lesson in the works with this story, and it strongly appears that Sarah understood this. It was the Lord who told Abraham to accept Sarah's proposal. Therefore, it was the Lord who taught the greater lesson in this story on the blessings of the eternal family and the Abrahamic covenant that makes it all possible.

The same God who told Abraham to listen to his wife and let Hagar and Ishmael go also reiterated a promise to Abraham regarding his posterity and the covenant. "But my covenant will I establish with Isaac, which Sarah shall bear unto thee" (Genesis 17:21). This covenant is the key difference between Isaac and Ishmael, as amplified in Ishmael's banishment with Hagar.

The message is clear: Isaac was the vehicle of the covenant and the promises made to Abraham decades before and reiterated through the ensuing years. In terms perhaps more familiar to us, Isaac was the child born in the covenant; Ishmael was not. Without the covenant carried through Isaac, Ishmael and Hagar could not be a part of Abraham's eternal family. "For if ye will not abide in my covenant ye are not worthy of me" (D&C 98:15).[52]

That is not to say that Abraham did not love Hagar or Ishmael, and it's not to say that the Lord did not love Hagar or Ishmael. Quite the contrary, the Lord's multiple visitations to Hagar show that he was mindful of her and Ishmael, as He is with all His children (Genesis 16:7–14; 21:17–21).

These were wonderful blessings; they just were not the fulness of the Lord's blessings. There is no mention of the priesthood in regards to Ishmael's children, nor of the stars in relation to Ishmael's posterity. For all of the conflict over whose land Canaan is through the millennia, there is no mention of the promised land for Ishmael's seed. And finally, as we see in this painful example, they did not stay together as a family.

All of those blessings were reserved for Isaac within the covenant. Those blessings belong to the fulness of the Lord and His priesthood. They belong to the temple.

Like many Old Testament examples, the separation of Abraham, Hagar, and Ishmael is a type—a symbol meant to convey a greater lesson. The Old Testament is filled with stories that seem harsh to us but are meant to convey gospel principles. For example, throughout the Old Testament and up to the time of Christ, countless innocent animals were slain and offered as sacrifices. All of this was to teach of the Lamb of God, who would be slain and offered for the sins of the world. Cutting the throat of a lamb and collecting its blood in a cup according to the law would be a most startling experience to us, no doubt. That is just the way the Lord planned it. That way, the lesson would leave a deep impression, sure to sink into the minds of all those participating and witnessing.

The Exodus story is packed with such types, as drastic as they may seem. To the Egyptians who held the Israelites captive, the Lord sent curses—waters changing to blood; infestations of frogs, lice, and flies; dying cattle; boils; flaming hail; locusts; and three days of darkness (Exodus 7–10). When this still did not convince Pharaoh to let the Lord's covenant people go, all the homes that did not apply the blood of a lamb to the entryway lost their firstborn (Exodus 12). These are dramatic examples, and that is perhaps the point. The physical destruction visited upon the Egyptians is a clear representation of the spiritual destruction of those who do not heed the call to repentance. It is an especially dramatic call to apply the atoning blood of the Savior in our homes and families, as we certainly do not want to lose any dear members of our families for eternity.

In a similar way, Abraham, Ishmael, and Hagar present a dramatic type, meant to convey a message on the marriage covenant. The covenant—the same covenant that promises the blessing of eternal families—was not with Ishmael and Hagar. They couldn't remain intact as a family for that reason. As hard as it was for them to do, and as heartless as Sarah and Abraham may appear to those who don't understand the deeper lesson, this story prefigures the family that does not embrace the covenants and ordinances necessary to stay together for eternity.

Again, this does not mean that the Lord does not love all His children or that He will not bless His children in many, many ways. We clearly have seen His love to Hagar and Ishmael. It is simply a lesson of eternal families and the Abrahamic covenant.

Ishmael was promised worldly blessings. Isaac was promised eternal blessings, including eternal families and everything that Abraham had. As the seed of Abraham, Isaac, and Jacob, we should choose the eternal blessings.

- *Following years of infertility, Sarah gave her handmaid Hagar to Abraham so that he might have children. This practice was in accordance with both the customs of the time and the Lord's commandment.*
- *Hagar bore Abraham a son, Ishmael.*
- *The Lord showed great love and concern for Hagar and promised great blessings to Ishmael and his seed. However, these blessings were earthly blessings and were not as great as the blessings promised to Abraham.*
- *The Lord made it clear that the covenant He had made with Abraham would be passed through Isaac.*
- *Even though Abraham and the Lord loved Hagar and Ishmael, the Lord did not permit them to remain with Abraham. This teaches us that even though the Lord loves all His children, and even though family members may love each other greatly, they cannot remain as an eternal unit without the sealing power exercised in the Abrahamic covenant.*

# Genesis 17

## New Names and Kings from Abraham's Seed

**A*t the age*** of ninety-nine, Abraham had another temple experience, recorded in Genesis 17. This was a temple experience because it further involved Abraham's covenant with the Lord, and that covenant is administered only in the temple. It also qualifies as a temple experience because Abraham received revelation from the Lord and was given divine instruction and divine laws. Like Genesis 15, there is no specific mention of an altar in chapter 17, but it is implied. One notable reference to an altar in Genesis 17 was the commandment of circumcision. This required the spilling of blood—human blood—in similitude of the animal sacrifices offered throughout the Old Testament on the altar in the temple. It was also a similitude of the blood of the Savior shed in Gethsemane and Golgotha.

### New Names for Abraham and Sarah

Immediately after the Lord appeared to Abraham and gave him commandments, Abraham "fell on his face," showing both humility and reverence for the Lord (Genesis 17:3). After this show of reverence, the Lord echoed familiar words to Abraham. "As for me, behold, my covenant is with thee, and thou shalt be a father of many nations" (Genesis 17:4). Abraham had heard that promise many times before over the decades. He was still waiting, ever faithfully, for that promise to be fulfilled.

This time, however, the Lord quickly followed the familiar promise with a new name for Abraham. "Neither shall thy name any more be called Abram, but thy name shall be Abraham; for a father of many nations have I made thee" (Genesis 17:5).

The Lord specifically included Sarah in this promise and also pronounced a new name for her. "And God said unto Abraham, As for Sarai thy wife, thou shalt not call her name Sarai, but Sarah shall her name be. And I will bless her, and give thee a son also of her: yea, I will bless her" (Genesis 17:15–16).

Both of the earthly partners in this covenant received new names as part of the covenant. Abraham's new name means "father of a multitude," and Sarah's means "princess."

## The Significance of New Names for Us

The blessing of a new name signifies a covenant relationship and may prefigure the blessings of that covenant. Names carried a particular importance in the Old Testament and in the Book of Mormon. A name was intended to teach lessons of a child's true identity and promise. We see this clearly in the book of Helaman. "Behold, my sons, I desire that ye should remember to keep the commandments of God; and I would that ye should declare unto the people these words. Behold, I have given unto you the names of our first parents who came out of the land of Jerusalem; and this I have done that when you remember your names ye may remember them; and when ye remember them ye may remember their works; and when ye remember their works ye may know how that it is said, and also written, that they were good" (Helaman 5:6).

"The Hebrew word *sem*, usually translated *name*, can also be rendered *remembrance* or *memorial*, indicating that the name acts as a reminder to its bearers and others. The name shows both the true nature of its bearer and the relationship that exists between people."[53]

*Smith's Bible Dictionary* teaches, "No monuments are more enduring than names. Sometimes they are the most ancient records of persons, places and things. They are fossils of thought. Bible names have almost always a meaning, which is often given by the writer for a purpose. The meaning of a name being known, we are able to get a better knowledge of persons and their history, especially if the name was given for some special reason or act."[54]

Understanding the ancient importance of names and their meanings, it makes perfect sense that a new name, such as Abraham and Sarah were given, would be received as a result of a covenant. The nature of the bearer and his or her relationship to God necessarily changes upon entering into a covenant with God. Likewise, as *Smith's* teaches, the enduring legacy of a person would clearly be based on a covenant that would bring endless posterity, eternal priesthood, and an inheritance with God. The "special reason or act" for this new name would begin with the covenant.

Names were officially given to boys after circumcision, an event referencing both a covenant and an ordinance, probably for this same reason (see Luke 1:59; 2:21). The name was tied with the covenant and formed a hope for the child's identity and righteousness.

## New Names Prefiguring of Covenant Blessings

Both Abraham and Sarah's new names represent great honors, no doubt, and both may also prefigure greater eternal blessings. As heirs to the Abrahamic covenant, those blessings prefigured by Abraham and Sarah's new names are also lessons and promises to us.

Sarah's new name means "princess." What is a princess? She is a queen in waiting. She, born into royalty, and her destiny is to reign one day. Abraham's new name means "father of a multitude." This title could apply to either his mortal offspring or his eternal role in light of the blessings promised that go beyond mortality.

With both Sarah and Abraham, the process of receiving a new name points beyond mortality and into eternity. It is a prefiguring of blessings that await them.

A continuing parallel between Abraham and Adam, also involving the blessing of a new name, is evident in Doctrine and Covenants

107. This section is a lesson on the patriarchal order of the priesthood that Abraham had sought and, by now, received (D&C 107:40). In this account, Adam called together his righteous posterity and bestowed upon them "his last blessing" (D&C 107:53). Upon receiving this blessing, "the Lord appeared unto them, and they rose up and blessed Adam, and called him Michael, the prince, the archangel" (D&C 107:54).

Michael wasn't Adam's name in mortality, yet this is the name his posterity called him as they reflected on his priesthood and dealings with them as a patriarch. "And the Lord administered comfort unto Adam, and said unto him: I have set thee to be at the head; a multitude of nations shall come of thee, and thou art a prince over them forever" (D&C 107:55). These blessings pronounced by the Lord to Adam should sound familiar, as they are some of the same ones promised to Abraham. Something about this great occasion linked the eternal blessings of the Abrahamic covenant with a new name, in Adam's case.

Michael is the name by which Adam is known in his postmortal existence (see Doctrine and Covenants 78:16). Joseph Smith taught that Michael, which means "who is like God," also happens to be the name given to Adam in the premortal life, where he obtained the priesthood "in the Creation before the world was formed."[55]

In Adam's case, this new name represented both his divine origin and destiny. In both cases, the name *Michael* represented his nature of being like God.

In a similar manner, some rabbis believe that Abraham's new name represented God giving of Himself to Abraham. The *he* (pronounced "hey") is a letter from the name Jehovah, indicating that the Lord gave a part of His name to Abraham through this covenant.[56] This represented the Lord sharing His glory, powers, and blessings through the power of covenant.

By modern revelation, we know that the great patriarch Noah is the angel Gabriel.[57] This postmortal name means "man of God." Other angels listed in scripture include Raphael (mentioned in D&C 128:21), Uriel, Raguel, Sariel, and Jerahmeel, found in the apocryphal book of Enoch. The last three of these were also given other names: Izidiel, Hanael, and Kepharel.[58] All these angels have theomorphic names, ending with the Hebrew suffix *el*, meaning "God," indicating that they have a special relationship with Him. At least three of these angels are mentioned by two different names. This means they received a new name at some point.

Of all these examples, the Adam new name paradigm is perhaps the most instructive to us. Like Adam, we came from the presence of God. We are His spirit children. We were like Him—as evidenced in Adam's new name, Michael, meaning "who is like God"—in the premortal existence because He is the Father of our spirits. We came to earth as mankind, as evidenced by Adam's name, which literally means "mankind." We have the potential to become like God in the postmortal world through the blessings of the Atonement. The blessing of a new name to Adam represents the blessings available to all of us as sons and daughters of God.

Abraham's experience in receiving a new name followed this same covenant pattern. He received the name as a result of his covenant with God, and his new name represented his divine and eternal promise. As children of Abraham, the same blessing and personal message await us.

## Taking upon Ourselves the Name of Christ

Receiving a new name as a result of a covenant should not be a foreign concept to us by any means. We take upon ourselves the name of Christ when we enter the waters of baptism. This is a new name. This name isn't formally added to birth certificates or identification, but we bear the name because of the covenant we have made to follow Him.

The men who endure in the covenant of baptism are blessed to receive the Melchizedek Priesthood. This priesthood was originally titled the Holy Priesthood, after the order of the Son of God, but its name was changed to protect the sanctity of the Savior's name (D&C 107:3–4). Understanding the original and true name of this priesthood, those who receive it also take upon themselves the name of Christ in another symbolic but real way.

When we have endured righteously and long enough under the covenant of baptism and, for the men, the covenant of the Melchizedek

Priesthood, we receive higher ordinances and enter into higher covenants in the temple. This is likely where the practice of a wife taking on her husband's last name began. This practice follows the same pattern of a new name being received as part of a higher covenant of devotion, fidelity, and service. "It is through covenants and the reception of a new name that individuals are adopted into the family of the Lord and are eligible to be redeemed."[59]

Taking the name of the Savior upon us is a poignant reference to the Atonement. Think of the Savior bearing the weight of all the sins that you and I have ever committed *and* all the pain that we have ever felt (see Isaiah 53:4–5). In Gethsemane, the weight of this sacrifice was so overwhelming, so incomprehensible, that it literally crushed the blood from the Savior, driving it out through every pore in His body, as if His flesh were torn.

Now imagine Him the next day on the cross. Here, He suffered the pains of Gethsemane all over again. Before He was even lifted up on the cross, His flesh was punctured by a thorny "crown" and His back was shredded by a whip. Now, on the cross, His flesh was literally torn, pierced by nails in His hands, wrists, and feet and gouged in His side by a spear.

In both instances, He was not just suffering and bleeding; He was suffering and bleeding for us. He was bearing not just the weight of our sins, but of every sorrow, grief, and heartbreak we could ever suffer in mortality.

In Gethsemane, He suffered in completely voluntarily. No one drove nails through His flesh. No one committed a specific act to Him. We all bear grief and sorrow in mortality, and not always as a result of our own sins or choices; such are simply a part of mortality. None of us can teach the Savior anything about suffering through this kind of heartbreak. He already suffered for us in Gethsemane.

On the cross, the Savior bled and died because of direct choices, premeditated actions, and unmistakable wickedness, all from others. It was the definite and direct sin of mankind that placed the Savior on the cross and, soon thereafter, in the tomb. True, it was the Roman soldiers who drove the nails through His flesh, but there was no shortage of blame for the acts that placed Him upon the cross. And there is no shortage of beneficiaries of the Savior's sacrifice. It was for our sins, iniquities, and imperfections that the Savior bled and died.

Between Gethsemane and Golgotha, the complete debt of mortality—sorrows and sins alike—was paid.

Now consider that, for some undefined but real period of time, the Savior suffered specifically for each of us. For some period of time in that unspeakable agony that eventually claimed His mortal life, the Savior's actions were for you alone.

For some period of time, the Savior must have taken upon Himself our individual names as He took upon Himself our sins and sorrows. That act of taking each of us individually and distinctively upon Himself allows each of us the blessings of forgiveness and eternal life through obedience to the laws and ordinances of the gospel. It gives us new life, even eternal life.

We take upon ourselves His name, as in the ordinance of baptism, because He took upon Himself our sins and, in a real way, our names. This act of taking upon ourselves the name of the Jesus Christ, the Son of God, follows the covenants that allow us to become His children through the Atonement. We take upon ourselves the Savior's name to receive the blessings of the Savior's taking upon Himself our sins or, symbolically, our names.

## "Kings Shall Come out of Thee"

The promise of posterity was renewed again in Genesis 17, though this time with another significant expansion on it. "And I will make thee exceeding fruitful, and I will make nations of thee, and kings shall come out of thee" (Genesis 17:6). This promise was fulfilled to Abraham, as the line of the great kings of Israel was born through his lineage (Matthew 1:1–17). Of course, by far, the greatest fulfillment of this promise was that the King of Kings, Jesus Christ, would be born of Abraham's lineage (see Bible Dictionary, "Abrahamic covenant").

To Abraham, this would be an overwhelming blessing. The Savior of all mankind, the Mediator of this great covenant with Abraham, would be born through him!

## This Blessing to Us: Becoming Sons and Daughters of Christ

We know the blessings promised to Abraham are promised to us as well, but the Savior could only be born one time in mortality. It may appear that this blessing promised to Abraham—of the King of Kings being part of his literal seed—has no modern-day application. How could it, as Jesus has already been born? But this blessing is most definitely available to us. Instead of Jesus Christ being born into our lineages, this blessing of the covenant is that we may be born spiritually through the Savior. This is a most precious blessing. It is the entire purpose of the Atonement, and it is a blessing of the Abrahamic covenant available to all of us.

Joseph Fielding Smith taught of this blessing received in the temple. Speaking of those who reject temple blessings, he taught, "They are not sons, they are not daughters. They are children of God, it is true, for all men are his children. But they do not inherit, and therefore remain servants throughout all eternity because they were not willing to receive that which they might have received, and the gift which was bestowed upon them or offered to them."[60] The key here is *inheritance*. Sons and daughters have a right to inherit from their father. In this case, that right is to inherit all that our Father has (D&C 84:38; Luke 15:31). That is the purpose and culmination of the Abrahamic covenant.

King Benjamin taught of the process of one becoming a son or daughter of Christ. When he gave his great conference address, those who heard it were overcome with the Holy Ghost. They experienced a might change of heart, a spiritual rebirth. This in turn led them to enter into a covenant to do the will of the Father "and to be obedient to his commandments in all things that he shall command" (Mosiah 5:5).

And in response to this mighty change of heart and covenant "to be obedient . . . in all things that he shall command," King Benjamin pronounced a great blessing on them. "Ye have spoken the words that I desired; and the covenant which ye have made is a righteous covenant.

And now, because of the covenant which ye have made ye shall be called the children of Christ, his sons, and his daughters; for behold, this day he hath spiritually begotten you; for ye say that your hearts are changed through faith on his name; therefore, ye are born of him and have become his sons and his daughters" (Mosiah 5:5–7).

Abinadi further taught about becoming a son and a daughter of Christ, speaking of His "seed."

> And now I say unto you, who shall declare his generation? Behold, I say unto you, that when his soul has been made an offering for sin he shall see his seed. And now what say ye? And who shall be his seed?
>
> Behold I say unto you, that whosoever has heard the words of the prophets, yea, all the holy prophets who have prophesied concerning the coming of the Lord—I say unto you, that all those who have hearkened unto their words, and believed that the Lord would redeem his people, and have looked forward to that day for a remission of their sins, I say unto you, that these are his seed, or they are the heirs of the kingdom of God.
>
> For these are they whose sins he has borne; these are they for whom he has died, to redeem them from their transgressions. And now, are they not his seed?
>
> Yea, and are not the prophets, every one that has opened his mouth to prophesy, that has not fallen into transgression, I mean all the holy prophets ever since the world began? I say unto you that they are his seed.
>
> And these are they who have published peace, who have brought good tidings of good, who have published salvation; and said unto Zion: Thy God reigneth!
>
> And O how beautiful upon the mountains were their feet!
>
> And again, how beautiful upon the mountains are the feet of those that are still publishing peace!
>
> And again, how beautiful upon the mountains are the feet of those who shall hereafter publish peace, yea, from this time henceforth and forever!
>
> And behold, I say unto you, this is not all. For O how beautiful upon the mountains are the feet of him that bringeth good tidings, that is the founder of peace, yea, even the Lord, who has redeemed his people; yea, him who has granted salvation unto his people. (Mosiah 15:10–18)

From these scriptures, we learn several of the characteristics of those who become sons and daughters of Christ.

First, they are spiritually reborn. They lose any desire to do evil and only want to do good continually (Mosiah 5:2). Second, they enter into a covenant to be obedient to the Lord in all things (Mosiah 5:5). Third, they have lived by every word of God given through His prophets (Mosiah 15:11). Fourth, they have received a complete forgiveness of their sins (Mosiah 15:12). This blessing in particular is what we seek. As we will see, the power and blessings from this covenant flow from the act of being cleansed from sin. Fifth, they have become prophets themselves. This blessing is not out of our reach; the testimony of Jesus is the spirit of prophecy. Those who inherit the celestial kingdom are valiant in this testimony (D&C 76:79). This is a gift of the Holy Ghost, which is the most priceless gift that we can receive in mortality. Sixth, they bear testimony. They are teachers and missionaries who gladly share their testimonies of the Savior. Seventh, they are temple attendees. Mountains are scriptural representations of the temple. The many references to mountains in Abinadi's discourse are no coincidence. Temple work is the most ennobling work in mortality. And eighth, they have walked in righteousness. Abinadi referred to feet often in these scriptures, just as he referred to mountains. Our feet are our method of walking, and walking represents the way we live our everyday lives. Our feet will be found beautiful (meaning clean) upon the mountains (the temple) as we are worthy to offer service and walk in the ways of the Lord.

All of these are references to the Abrahamic covenant, both in the works of the covenant and in its blessings. The fulness of these blessings can only be had in the temple. We can only be cleansed from all our sins through the blessings of the temple. Our full and complete spiritual rebirth is found in the temple. The covenant to be obedient to everything the Lord commands is found in the temple. Even missionary work is found in the temple, as the Lord has instructed missionaries to be "endowed with power from on high" before departing on missions (D&C 38:38; 43:16; 105:11).

Unlike Abraham, the Savior won't be born through our lines. But *we* may be born through *Him*. And that is another precious and beautiful gift of the Abrahamic covenant. It is no coincidence that this blessing comes in the same experience as Abraham's new name. A child born into this world bears the name of his father. By entering into the Abrahamic covenant, we take upon ourselves a new name, the name of our new spiritual father, Jesus Christ. Such are the blessings of the Atonement made possible through the Abrahamic covenant.

- *Abraham and Sarah both received new names as part of the Abrahamic covenant. Abraham's new name means "father of a multitude," and Sarah's means "princess."*
- *New names are associated with the covenant process and are symbolic of the new birth and relationship with God that comes through entering into covenants with Him.*
- *In Abraham and Sarah's case in particular, their new names appear to prefigure blessings of the covenant that they had been promised. For Sarah, the new name may have prefigured her ultimate crowning as a queen, consistent with the blessings of the Abrahamic covenant. For Abraham, the new name may have also prefigured the blessings of eternal posterity promised to him.*
- *In the saving ordinances of the gospel and the Abrahamic covenant, we also take upon ourselves a new name—the name of Jesus Christ.*
- *As the Savior suffered in Gethsemane and Golgotha, He took upon Himself our sins and sorrows and, symbolically, our names. That act leads to our forgiveness and eternal lives. We take upon ourselves His name as a similitude of the Savior's sacrifice for us.*
- *As another blessing of the Abrahamic covenant, Abraham was promised that kings would be born of him. This included the King of Kings, Jesus Christ.*
- *Through this covenant, we can be spiritually reborn through the Savior, becoming His spiritual sons and daughters.*
- *The Book of Mormon teaches that this process of becoming a spiritual son or daughter of Christ comes through covenant. The sons and daughters of Christ experience a mighty change of heart and are cleansed completely from their sins, enter into a covenant to obey every commandment from the Lord and live by every word from His prophets, are valiant in service (particularly in missionary and temple work), and are described as having beautiful feet upon the mountains.*
- *Feet are associated with walking, which is symbolic of the way we live our everyday lives. Mountains are symbolic of the temple. Therefore,*

*these references are symbolic of having lived worthily to enter and receive the blessings of the temple and giving service there.*

- *All of these blessings are found in the temple.*

# Genesis 18

## "For I Know Him"

**G*enesis 18 tells*** the familiar story of Abraham negotiating with the Lord over Sodom and Gomorrah. It doesn't contain any revelation on the blessings of the Abrahamic covenant, strictly speaking. But right in the middle of the chapter is perhaps the hidden gem of the Abrahamic covenant. The Lord revealed to the messengers He sent to administer to Abraham and Sarah the reason why He was willing to promise such great blessings to Abraham. This is a priceless insight for us, as we seek the same blessings. Here, the Lord said where our hearts need to be to qualify for these blessings. "And the men rose up from thence, and looked toward Sodom: and Abraham went with them to bring them on the way. And the Lord said, Shall I hide from Abraham that thing which I do; seeing that Abraham shall surely become a great and mighty nation, and all the nations of the earth shall be blessed in him?" (Genesis 18:16–18).

Now we will to tap directly into the Lord's thought process in this conversation with His messengers: "For I know him, that he will command his children and his household after him, and they shall keep the way of the Lord, to do justice and judgment; that the Lord may bring upon Abraham that which he hath spoken of him" (Genesis 18:19).

The Lord knew He could trust Abraham with the blessings of the covenant because Abraham would teach his children and those with him the ways of righteousness.

This brings a few scriptures to mind. First, "The Family: A Proclamation to the World." It reads in pertinent part:

> Husband and wife have a solemn responsibility to love and care for each other and for their children. "Children are an heritage of the Lord" (Psalm 127:3). Parents have a sacred duty to rear their children in love and righteousness, to provide for their physical and spiritual needs, and to teach them to love and serve one another, observe the commandments of God, and be law-abiding citizens wherever they live. Husbands and wives—mothers and fathers—will be held accountable before God for the discharge of these obligations.[61]

This divinely inspired proclamation is one of three doctrinal statements ever given by the First Presidency and the Quorum of the Twelve Apostles. It is a spiritual treasure, clearly stating our obligations as parents to teach our children and rear them in love and righteousness. The worth of a soul is great in the Lord's sight. These are the same qualifications for the blessings of the Abrahamic covenant.

Second, the parable of the talents. This parable concluded with the overseer's approbation of those who had magnified their talents: "Well done, thou good and faithful servant: thou hast been faithful over a few things, I will make thee ruler over many things: enter thou into the joy of thy lord" (Matthew 25:21). These are the same words we all hope to hear at Judgment Day. Abraham proved his loyalty in watching over a few things—namely, his household—so the Lord knew that He could trust Abraham to be a ruler over endless posterity.

Third, Sister Sheri L. Dew's landmark discourse "Are We Not All Mothers?"[62] The Lord was willing to bless Abraham not just for teaching his children righteousness, but also "his household after him" (Genesis 18:19). Who exactly was Abraham's household? It included everyone in Abraham's stewardship. If Abraham were a Primary teacher, he would have taught his Primary children beautifully, consistently, and lovingly because they were part of his stewardship. If he had been a deacons quorum advisor, that would have been one incredibly blessed deacons quorum. Much like Helaman and his two thousand warriors, whom he called his sons, those within our stewardship are our household, if not our children.

This is the same doctrine taught by Sister Dew, specifically to the Sarahs of the world. "Every one of us can mother someone—beginning, of course, with the children in our own families but extending far beyond. Every one of us can show by word and by deed that the work of women in the Lord's kingdom is magnificent and holy. I repeat: *We are all mothers in Israel,* and our calling is to love and help lead the rising generation through the dangerous streets of mortality."[63]

When the Lord knows that He can trust you with your own family and those in your household, whether they're your blood or not, then He will be able to trust you with so much more.

- *Genesis 18:19 is not a direct blessing of the Abrahamic covenant, but it does explain clearly why the Lord was willing to trust Abraham with the great blessings of the covenant.*
- *By teaching our children and those within our household or stewardship, we qualify for the same blessings as Abraham.*
- *This sacred duty is made clear in "The Family: A Proclamation to the World," the parable of the talents, and a landmark address by Sister Sheri L. Dew, all of which remind us that we have nurturing responsibilities, just as Abraham and Sarah did.*

# Genesis 22

## "By Myself Have I Sworn, Saith the Lord"

**Genesis 22 is** the deeply poignant account of Abraham taking his son Isaac up to Mount Moriah, where Abraham was commanded to offer him as a sacrifice. Known in religious circles as the *akedah*, or "the binding," I believe this to be the most significant chapter of scripture in the entire Old Testament.

As Abraham lifted the knife to offer the sacrifice, both Abraham and Isaac were spared when an angel intervened and told Abraham that his willingness to offer the sacrifice was enough. Abraham was spared the loss of his son. Isaac was spared his life. And yet another reiteration of the blessings of the Abrahamic covenant was promised. The angel taught Abraham, "By myself have I sworn, saith the Lord, for because thou hast done this thing, and hast not withheld thy son, thine only son: that in blessing I will bless thee, and in multiplying I will multiply thy seed as the stars of the heaven, and as the sand which is upon the sea shore; and thy seed shall possess the gate of his enemies; and in thy seed shall all the nations of the earth be blessed; because thou hast obeyed my voice" (Genesis 22:16–18).

These promises are familiar. Abraham had heard them several different times throughout his life, spanning many decades. The first several times Abraham heard these or similar promises, Isaac was just a dream. By now, Isaac was at least twenty-five. In this latest iteration of these blessings, the substance of the promises grew somewhat, yet the account of Genesis 22 actually represents an entirely different level of blessings to Abraham.

## The Sanctuary of the Covenant

The temple references in Genesis 22 are overwhelming. There's no question this was a temple experience for Abraham. First, Abraham and Isaac traveled up a mountain, which is the ubiquitous symbol of a temple in the scriptures. A mountain is the closest place to heaven on earth, where heaven meets earth. This particular mountain, Mount Moriah, was where the temple of Solomon would later be built (see 2 Chronicles 3:1). This is no coincidence. This was not just *a* temple experience; it was *the* temple experience of the entire Old Testament.

Adding to the temple experience was the altar upon which Isaac was offered but spared, and then where the ram caught in the thicket was offered instead (Genesis 22:9, 13).

Understanding Mount Moriah to be the most profound Old Testament temple, it's clear something extremely sacred and monumental was about to take place there.

## Sand on the Seashore

The promised blessings to Abraham this time contained several nuances, just as they did in previous iterations.

In Genesis 12, the promise of Abraham's seed was that he would become a great nation (Genesis 12:2). In Genesis 13, this promised seed was compared to the dust of the earth (Genesis 13:16). In Genesis 15, Abraham's promised seed was likened to the stars in the heavens (Genesis 15:5). In Genesis 17, the promise took the form of many nations and being multiplied exceedingly (Genesis 17:2, 4).

Here, the promise was given using the simile of sand on the seashore and stars in the heavens in addition to the same iteration of being multiplied greatly (Genesis 22:17). The Lord used the stars to describe

Abraham's posterity in Genesis 15, teaching us that the blessing would be fulfilled in the eternities. Here on Mount Moriah, both earthly and heavenly posterity—both sand and stars—were promised.

What is the difference between dust in Genesis 13 and sand on the seashore in Genesis 22? Both are impossible to count. Both represent hyperbole and infinity. If there is a difference between dust and sand, it's that sand on the seashore is close to water. Water is perhaps the most precious commodity in life. It gives and sustains life. Because of this, water is a scriptural emblem of covenant, which gives life (Moses 6:59–60). This particular body of water—the sea—is where the vast majority of water on the earth is found. It is also where the majority of salt—itself a great scriptural symbol of covenant, preservation, and righteousness—is found.

With the proximity of water referenced in Genesis 22, this blessing may have prefigured that Abraham's seed will have life and the blessings of the covenant on earth. It may also be that the dust of the earth earlier promised referred to Abraham's seed through Ishmael. No doubt, they would be great and innumerable, but they would not enjoy the blessings of the fulness, the blessings of the Abrahamic covenant. They would remain as dust—dry and waterless—while Abraham's seed through Isaac would be close to water, the Living Water, Jesus Christ (see John 4:13–14).

We are Abraham's seed through Isaac and Jacob. We've been blessed with the living waters of the Savior's restored gospel. This promised blessing is to us.

## "And Thy Seed Shall Possess the Gate of His Enemies"

In Genesis 22, the Lord added a new promise to Abraham regarding his seed. "And thy seed shall possess the gate of his enemies" (Genesis 22:17). Some biblical scholars have interpreted this to mean Abraham's descendants would be favored in their wars. While this may be true, there is more to this promise and its relation to the Abrahamic covenant.

There are two possible insights that seem to make sense. The first likely interpretation of this phrase draws from Joseph Smith's definition of salvation. "Salvation is nothing more nor less than to triumph over all our enemies and put them under our feet. And when we have power to put all enemies under our feet in this world, and a knowledge to triumph over all evil spirits in the world to come, then we are saved, as in the case of Jesus, who was to reign until He had put all enemies under His feet, and the last enemy was death."[64]

One "enemy" that Joseph contemplated in this definition was death. Physical death is not the only "enemy" the Savior defeats through the Atonement; the Savior's Atonement also defeats spiritual death, and, finally, the enemy of all righteousness (see 2 Nephi 9:4–13). These three are the ultimate enemies, and the Savior decimates them all.

In this light, the seed of Abraham having power to possess the gate of their enemies harkens back to the promises made to Adam and Eve when they were cast out of Eden. The Lord promised Adam and Eve that their seed would be *protected* by enmity. Specifically, the Lord gave Adam and Eve's seed or posterity the power to bruise or, more correctly translated, "crush" Satan's head (Genesis 3:15). In this same declaration, Satan's power was limited to the heel of Adam and Eve's seed. (The same Hebrew word for *bruise* is used in this phrase as well.) I personally would much rather have an exposed heel than a crushable head.

Understanding that the Prophet Joseph viewed salvation as triumphing over enemies (likely referring to physical and spiritual death and the enemy of all righteousness), the blessing of Abraham possessing the gate of his enemies could mean simply that Abraham's seed would gain salvation. This certainly fits with the blessings of the covenant.

Another possible meaning of this phrase comes from an alternate translation of the Bible, the Literal Translation (LIT). In that translation, two words are capitalized. "And thy *Seed* shall possess the gate of *His* enemies" (emphasis added). This suggests that Abraham's seed specifically meant the Savior.

If Abraham's seed is a specific reference to the Savior, that is certainly one way that the whole earth and the families upon it would be blessed by Abraham's "Seed." But it isn't the only possible correct interpretation of Abraham's seed. As it appears over the course of the scriptures, the phrase necessarily refers to all of Abraham's posterity, not just the Savior. However, it is still possible that Abraham's seed has a dual meaning, referring both to the Savior and to those who have entered into the Abrahamic covenant.

This dual meaning actually deepens our appreciation and understanding of the Atonement. The Savior has the ultimate power over Satan and his followers. He possesses the gate—symbolizing the power to come and go—of the enemies. He possesses the power of salvation, as Joseph Smith defined it.

He *shares* that power with the seed of Abraham through the Atonement. He gives His sons and daughters power over the enemies of physical and spiritual death through the Atonement. The seed of Abraham (you and I) access that power of the Savior (the "Seed" of Abraham) through the Abrahamic covenant. The Atonement becomes real and personal through the Abrahamic covenant, which binds us to God.

## The Oath in Genesis 22

To this point, our discussion has focused on the blessings of the Abrahamic covenant. These are the promises from the Lord, within the framework of biblical covenants discussed earlier. Genesis 22 introduces another important component of a covenant—the oath. It is this oath that gives the blessings of the covenant promised in Genesis 22 a whole new life.

Notice the introduction by the Lord when reiterating the promised blessings discussed above: "By myself have I sworn, saith the Lord, for because thou hast done this thing, and hast not withheld thy son, thine only son" (Genesis 22:16).

As we just saw, the blessings then promised to Abraham were largely the same as the blessings promised decades earlier. The difference with this iteration of the blessings was found in the introductory language of the Lord's oath, or "swearing" these blessings this time. This is the first mention of an oath in connection with these promises. Before, the blessings were given to Abraham as a promise to be received at some time in the future. This time, the blessings were given with an oath, making them immutable and irrevocable, as if personally guaranteed by the Lord.[65] With this oath, any conditions previously associated with the promises to Abraham were removed.

The circumstances of Genesis 22 give further evidence that this promise was distinctly different from the previous occasions. For example, Abraham had to pass tests of faith and obedience after each of the previous promises. Genesis 22, however, is the last of the promises given to Abraham in the scriptures. As we will examine in the next section of this book, it is also the last of divine laws—the last of the "works of Abraham"—that the Lord asked of him. Here, Abraham fulfilled all of the commandments of the Lord. Here, the Lord removed any condition associated with the promises. Abraham passed all of the tests, and there were no more conditions to be fulfilled. The blessings of eternal life were now assured to Abraham while still in mortality.

Here again, the oath and covenant of the priesthood are evident (D&C 84:39–40). This time, it was not just promised but fulfilled. The oath sworn by the Lord on Mount Moriah is in fact the oath to give all the Father hath (D&C 84:38).

It is the fulness of the priesthood sealed and fulfilled. We spoke of invitations from modern-day prophets to strive for these blessings, but this invitation in the Doctrine and Covenants is the most open and obvious of all such invitations.

Abraham had now received the fulness of the priesthood blessings he had sought from the beginning.

## Abraham's Calling and Election Made Sure

The oath from the Lord sealing Abraham's promised blessings on Mount Moriah constitutes the greatest blessing one can receive in mortality. Eternal life is the greatest gift of God (D&C 14:7). The Lord has provided a way to receive an assurance of that blessing while still in mortality, and Abraham is the most complete example we have of this process. In this sense, the Judgment Day may be advanced to mortality, and faithful Saints may receive the assurance of being, not just the conditional promise of becoming. This is referred to as having one's calling and election made sure (see 2 Peter 1:10). This is also the "more sure word of prophecy" mentioned in Doctrine and Covenants 131:5.

The Prophet Joseph Smith taught extensively on this subject, continually exhorting the early Saints to strive for the blessing of having their calling and election made sure. Expounding on 2 Peter 1, where Peter introduced the phrase of having one's calling and election made sure, Joseph taught,

> Now, there is some grand secret here, and keys to unlock the subject. Notwithstanding the apostle exhorts them to add to their faith, virtue, knowledge, temperance, &c., yet he exhorts them to make their calling and election sure. And though they had heard an audible voice from heaven bearing testimony that Jesus was the Son of God, yet he says we have a more sure word of prophecy, whereunto ye do well that ye take heed as unto a light shining in a dark place. Now, wherein could they have a more sure word of prophecy than to hear the voice of God saying, This is my beloved Son.
>
> Now for the secret and grand key. Though they might hear the voice of God and know that Jesus was the Son of God, this would be no evidence that their [calling and election] was made sure, that they had part with Christ, and were joint heirs with him. They then would want that more sure word of prophecy, that they were sealed in the heavens and had the promise of eternal life in the kingdom of God. Then, having this promise sealed unto them, it was an anchor to the soul, sure and steadfast.[66]

After explaining this doctrine, Joseph Smith openly invited the Saints to strive for this blessing of having the Lord advance their Judgment Day and seal upon them their eternal lives while yet in mortality. "Then I would exhort you to go on and continue to call upon God until you make your calling and election sure for yourselves, by obtaining this more sure word of prophecy, and wait patiently for the promise until you obtain it."[67]

Through the years, the Prophet became even more enthusiastic and downright urgent with the Saints as he continued to teach this doctrine. "Oh! I beseech you to go forward, go forward and make your calling and your election sure."[68]

This same urging for us to make our calling and election sure has been restated by prophets and Apostles throughout this dispensation. Notably, President Benson echoed this same plea in 1985.

> God bless us to teach our children and our grandchildren what great blessings temple attendance brings. God bless us to receive all the blessings that await us by going to the temple. God bless us to receive all the blessings revealed by Elijah the prophet so that our callings and elections will be made sure.
>
> I testify with all my soul to the truth of this message and pray that the God of Abraham, Isaac, and Jacob will bless modern Israel with the compelling desire to seek all the blessings of the fathers in the house of our Heavenly Father.[69]

Clearly, Abraham's experience on Mount Moriah of receiving the promise of exaltation while still in mortality is something that prophets, ancient and modern, have invited us to strive for. It isn't a blessing reserved for just prophets and Apostles. It is the most sacred of subjects, so it should be spoken of only in the most sacred of circumstances. It is clearly inappropriate to ask General Authorities anything personal on the subject, and we should take great care to avoid sensationalizing the subject. But we should still seek sacred experiences where the Spirit is present so that we can learn of it. Multiple prophets have urged us to work toward that goal. This is, after all, one of the works of Abraham that we are commanded to emulate.

## Following Abraham up Mount Moriah

Joseph Smith taught the Saints specifically and matter-of-factly how to work toward this blessing. His teachings seem to follow the example of Abraham exactly, as if Joseph had been reading the eleven chapters in Genesis in particular.

> After a person has faith in Christ, repents of his sins, and is baptized for the remission of his sins and receives the Holy Ghost (by the laying on of hands), which is the first Comforter, then let him continue to humble himself before God, hungering and thirsting after righteousness, and living by every word of God, and the Lord will soon say unto him, Son,

> thou shalt be exalted. When the Lord has thoroughly proved him, and finds that the man is determined to serve Him at all hazards, then the man will find his calling and his election made sure.[70]

By no coincidence, when the Lord Himself promised this assurance of exaltation on Joseph, making his calling and election sure, the Lord compared Joseph to Abraham and his offering of Isaac.

> For I am the Lord thy God, and will be with thee even unto the end of the world, and through all eternity; for verily I seal upon you your exaltation, and prepare a throne for you in the kingdom of my Father, with Abraham your father.
>
> Behold, I have seen your sacrifices, and will forgive all your sins; I have seen your sacrifices in obedience to that which I have told you. Go, therefore, and I make a way for your escape, as I accepted the offering of Abraham of his son Isaac. (D&C 132:49–50)

The event leading to the crowning of eternal life was Abraham's sacrifice of his son Isaac, as taught in Genesis 22. Abraham did not arrive at this point quickly or easily. Consider the steps that lead to the assurance of eternal life being received in mortality, as taught by Joseph Smith. Abraham's life exemplifies all of them to a tee.

Abraham's faith was proven throughout his life. It was manifest in his patience in waiting until his ninety-ninth year to be blessed with Isaac. It was shown from the beginning of his story in Genesis, where he heeded the word of the Lord to "get thee out of thy country, and from thy kindred, and from thy father's house, unto a land" that the Lord would show him (Genesis 12:1).

Abraham's forsaking of his sins was understood in his quest for "greater happiness and peace and rest" as he sought to go from being "a follower of righteousness" to becoming "a greater follower of righteousness" (Abraham 1:2).

The Bible doesn't speak specifically of Abraham's baptism and confirmation, but it is mentioned in the LDS Bible Dictionary and in the Talmud.[71]

Abraham showed his humility by constantly following God. We are given a specific example of this when he "fell on his face" when God spoke with him (Genesis 17:3).

Abraham's hunger and thirst after righteousness were clear from the beginning of his story. Abraham openly declared his desire to "be one who possessed great knowledge, and to be a greater follower of righteousness, and to possess a greater knowledge, and to be a father of many nations, a prince of peace, and desiring to receive instructions, and to keep the commandments of God" (Abraham 1:2).

Abraham's life was a perfect roadmap in accordance with Joseph Smith's instructions for receiving the assurance of eternal life while still in mortality.

In Genesis 22, Abraham proved that he was determined to serve the Lord at all costs. In asking Abraham to sacrifice his son, the Lord was thoroughly proving Abraham. Abraham had literally spent his life in pursuit of this blessing. Isaac represented the heart of everything Abraham wanted in life, and there was nothing unrighteous or selfish about this. Isaac was to be the means of carrying the covenant and all of its blessings promised to Abraham. No sacrifice, no commandment,could have been more anguishing or consuming for the Lord to request. In this sense, Isaac was the perfect measure of the dedication required to receive this greatest blessing of mortality: the assurance of eternal life.

The sacrifice of Isaac therefore perfectly embodies the level of dedication that Joseph Smith taught was necessary to have one's calling and election made sure. Likewise, the blessings promised to Abraham on that mountain that day are available to us as part of the Abrahamic covenant in the mountain (meaning temple) of the Lord today.

Abraham started his quest for the blessings of the covenant by seeking "greater happiness and peace and rest" (Abraham 1:2). On Mount Moriah (by no coincidence, where the great temple of Solomon was built; see 2 Chronicles 3:1), Abraham found the ultimate peace. He received the promise of eternal life and happiness and ultimate rest in the celestial kingdom. Abraham enjoyed the ultimate fulfillment of the Lord's promise that "he who doeth the works of righteousness shall receive his reward, even peace in this world, and eternal life in the world to come" (D&C 59:23). Knowing that we will receive eternal life was the ultimate peace in this world.

- *Abraham passed the ultimate test by proving his willingness to sacrifice what was most dear to him: his son Isaac.*
- *As a result of passing this test, the Lord reiterated the promises of the Abrahamic covenant, comparing Abraham's seed to the sand on the seashore in addition to the stars in the heavens promised earlier. This may be a reference to Abraham's seed having the blessings of the gospel, as shown by the proximity to water on the seashore.*
- *The Lord also added a promise that Abraham's seed would have power over the gate of his enemies. This refers to Abraham's seed having the blessings of salvation, as Joseph Smith defined it. It may also refer specifically to the Savior, as Abraham's "Seed."*
- *Under either interpretation, this is a reference to the Atonement. The blessing means that Abraham's seed would enjoy the blessings of the Atonement.*
- *The most notable difference between Genesis 22 and the other chapters promising blessings to Abraham is that this time the promised blessings were accompanied by an oath from the Lord, swearing that these promises would be realized.*
- *Oaths are recognized as making the promises of a covenant irrevocable and immutable. In this case, biblical scholars recognize this oath as the Lord's personal guarantee of these blessings to Abraham.*
- *Abraham's experience on Mount Moriah represented an advancement of Abraham's Judgment Day and a removal of any conditions on the promised blessings.*
- *This is a lesson on the doctrine of having one's calling and election made sure, a doctrine that has been taught by the Apostle Peter, Joseph Smith, and modern-day prophets.*
- *Briefly summarized, this doctrine is that our Judgment Day may be accelerated, and the blessings of eternal life may be sealed on us while still in mortality.*
- *These are blessings of the Abrahamic covenant that we have entered into in the temple. They are conditional and dependent on our faithfulness, but if we follow the example of Abraham, the Lord may remove the conditions and seal our exaltation on us while still in the flesh.*

# Genesis 24–48

## The Covenant Renewed through Isaac and Jacob

A***braham received and*** experienced the fulness of the blessings of the covenant in Genesis 22, where the Lord gave His oath sealing all of its blessings onto Abraham. But the lessons of the Abrahamic covenant have only begun for us. As declared from the beginning, the blessings of the covenant were not just for Abraham and Sarah but also for their family. Following Genesis 22, we see the true patriarchal nature of these blessings, as they were renewed through Abraham's family within the covenant, even down to us in the latter days. Here, we see that our God is not just the God of Abraham, but rather the God of Abraham, Isaac, and Jacob.

### The Covenant Renewed through Rebekah

Following Abraham and Isaac's experience on Mount Moriah, the covenant is first renewed through Rebekah, the wife chosen for Isaac by Abraham through his servant. "And they [Abraham's servant and his companions] blessed Rebekah, and said unto her, Thou art our sister, be thou the mother of thousands of millions, and let thy seed possess the gate of those which hate them" (Genesis 24:60). In this instance, it was not the Lord or the prophet Abraham who pronounced this blessing; it was Abraham's servant and "his men" (Genesis 24:59). Abraham's unnamed servant and his companions were sent by Abraham and were doing Abraham's will concerning the covenant to be carried through Isaac and Rebekah.

This seems to be an example of the Lord's pattern. He calls prophets, such as Abraham. Those prophets proclaim His word (Acts 10:39–43). Their voice is the same as His (D&C 1:38). The Holy Ghost confirms the words of the prophets (Acts 10:44). And those who hear are invited to obey by entering into a covenant (Acts 10:47–48).

Because Rebekah obeyed the prophet Abraham's word to enter into the celestial marriage covenant with Isaac, she was the first person beyond Abraham and Sarah to receive a promise of the blessings of the Abrahamic covenant.

## The Covenant Renewed through Isaac

Rebekah's companion in the marriage covenant, Isaac, received the promise of the same blessings. "And the Lord appeared unto [Isaac], and said, Go not down into Egypt; dwell in the land which I shall tell thee of" (Genesis 26:2). If this sounds familiar, it is because the Lord gave Isaac's father remarkably similar instructions years before (Genesis 12:1). The promises that followed should be familiar as well. "Sojourn in this land, and I will be with thee, and will bless thee; for unto thee, and unto thy seed, I will give all these countries, and I will perform the oath which I sware unto Abraham thy father; and I will make thy seed to multiply as the stars of heaven, and will give unto thy seed all these countries; and in thy seed shall all the nations of the earth be blessed" (Genesis 26:3–4).

Like Abraham, these promises were given in different experiences throughout Isaac's life, coupled with different commandments also given. Like Abraham, Isaac followed this first experience where the Lord gave him the promises of the covenant by seeking to save his wife's life. He even went about doing this the same way that Abraham spared Sarah—by telling covetous people smitten with Rebekah that she was his sister (Genesis 26:7). As He did for Abraham, the Lord blessed Isaac greatly (see Genesis 26:12–16).

Also like Abraham, Isaac received a separate visitation of the Lord, who repeated the promises of the covenant to Isaac. Though this second account is found in the same chapter, the experience is distinct and likely several years later. "And the Lord appeared unto [Isaac] the same night, and said, I am the God of Abraham thy father: fear not, for I am with thee, and will bless thee, and multiply thy seed for my servant Abraham's sake" (Genesis 26:24).

As with Abraham, this was a temple experience, as demonstrated by the altar where Isaac called on the name of the Lord (Genesis 26:25).

## The Covenant Renewed through Jacob

With Isaac's son Jacob, the covenant entered its third generation of this wondrous biblical lesson. The story of Isaac's first son, Esau, parallels the story of Abraham's first son, Ishmael. While Ishmael was born outside of the covenant, Esau chose to marry outside of the covenant, taking Judith, a Hittite (meaning Gentile), as his bride (Genesis 26:34). Genesis 26 teaches only that this was "a grief of mind unto Isaac and to Rebekah" (Genesis 26:35). As with Ishmael, the covenant of celestial inheritance, eternal priesthood, and eternal families could not pass through Esau because his ways ventured outside the covenant. There is the famous story of Esau selling his birthright for a mess of pottage in the preceding chapter, but it was Esau's choice to marry outside the covenant that gave Isaac and Rebekah true grief. No doubt, many of us sell our covenants for money, so to speak, but it is the Lord who ultimately gives and takes. It appears that marrying outside the covenant is the act that truly cost Esau his covenant rights in the eyes of the Lord.

Jacob, however, was righteous and lived within the covenant that was designed to make him and his family joint heirs with Christ of all that the Father has. Jacob first received a promise of the covenant blessings through his father, Isaac. Isaac blessed Jacob, "Therefore God give thee of the dew of heaven [as in, priesthood; see D&C 121:45], and the fatness of the earth, and plenty of corn and wine: let people serve thee, and nations bow down to thee: be lord over thy brethren, and let thy mother's sons bow down to thee: cursed be every one that curseth thee, and blessed be he that blesseth thee" (Genesis 27:28–29).

Again acting as a patriarch, Isaac later gave his son another blessing that encompassed the blessings of the Abrahamic covenant.

> And Isaac called Jacob, and blessed him, and charged him, and said unto him, Thou shalt not take a wife of the daughters of Canaan.
>
> Arise, go to Padan-aram, to the house of Bethuel thy mother's father; and take thee a wife from thence of the daughters of Laban thy mother's brother.
>
> And God Almighty bless thee, and make thee fruitful, and multiply thee, that thou mayest be a multitude of people;
>
> And give thee the blessing of Abraham, to thee, and to thy seed with thee; that thou mayest inherit the land wherein thou art a stranger, which God gave unto Abraham. (Genesis 28:1–4)

## Jacob's Temple Experience

The experience that followed this patriarchal blessing is one of the greatest temple experiences in all of scripture. Jacob followed the admonition of his father and went to find a righteous wife.

On his way, Jacob stopped to rest for the night and had a vision, in which he:

> [Beheld] a ladder set up on the earth, and the top of it reached to heaven: and behold the angels of God ascending and descending on it.
>
> And, behold, the Lord stood above it, and said, I am the Lord God of Abraham thy father, and the God of Isaac: the land whereon thou liest, to thee will I give it, and to thy seed;
>
> And thy seed shall be as the dust of the earth, and thou shalt spread abroad to the west, and to the east, and to the north, and to the south: and in thee and in thy seed shall all the families of the earth be blessed.
>
> And, behold, I am with thee, and will keep thee in all places whither thou goest, and will bring thee again into this land; for I will not leave thee, until I have done that which I have spoken to thee of. (Genesis 28:12–15)

Jacob himself declared this a temple experience. "Surely the Lord is in this place; and I knew it not. . . . This is none other but the house of God, and this is the gate of heaven" (Genesis 28:16–17). Jacob even called the place Beth-el, meaning "house of God" (Genesis 28:19). He poured oil at the site of his dream, indicating the place was holy and consecrated (Genesis 28:18).

Like anyone appropriately moved by a temple experience, Jacob left determined to take the experience with him and live his life in a way that would merit the blessings promised to him. "And Jacob vowed a vow, saying, If God will be with me, and will keep me in this way that I go, and will give me bread to eat, and raiment to put on, so that I come again to my father's house in peace; then shall the Lord be my God: and this stone, which I have set for a pillar, shall be God's house: and of all that thou shalt give me I will surely give the tenth unto thee" (Genesis 28:20–22).

Jacob's temple experience depicts our own temple experience. He was given to see a ladder reaching all the way from earth to heaven, bridging the gap between this life and the next, crossing the canyon between the world and the celestial. The rungs on that ladder provided for angels to descend to earth and minister and to ascend back to heaven, carrying precious cargo. According to President Marion G. Romney, the rungs on Jacob's ladder are representative of, quite simply, the ordinances and covenants of the temple.[72]

The Prophet Joseph Smith took the imagery one step further, relating Jacob's ladder to the three degrees of glory. "Paul ascended into the third heavens, and he could understand the three principal rounds of Jacob's ladder—the telestial, the terrestrial, and the celestial glories or kingdoms."[73] Overlapping these prophetic statements, the rungs on Jacob's ladder represent the ordinances and covenants of the temple, and those rungs ascend through three principal rounds, one representing the telestial kingdom, the second representing the terrestrial, and the highest representing the celestial.

This is one of the most beautiful expressions of the Abrahamic covenant. Jacob received the promises of the Abrahamic covenant through a vision while he beheld the angels we can't see ascending and descending to take Heavenly Father's children back to His presence. He also saw quite clearly the path that we have to follow to reach that destination, the path of covenants and ordinances that ultimately leads to the celestial kingdom. And finally, Jacob recognized that this vision, this understanding, and this ladder to heaven are all part of the temple.

## Jacob Received a New Name

Jacob's temple experience at Beth-el was not the end of his journey. Remember, he was on his way to find his wife when he had this experience. Jacob had now received the promises of the Abrahamic covenant in a patriarchal blessing from his father and in his temple experience at Beth-el. He still had decades of service and obedience before those blessings would be sealed on him by the Lord's oath.

Several years after Genesis 28, Jacob returned to Beth-el, where the Lord had appeared unto him and promised him the blessings of the covenant. There, Jacob built an altar, as the Lord had instructed him (Genesis 35:1, 6–7). This was Jacob's most recent temple experience. Like his grandfather, Jacob received a new name in this temple experience. "And God said unto him, Thy name is Jacob: thy name shall not be called any more Jacob, but Israel shall be thy name: and he called his name Israel" (Genesis 35:10).

With this new name, meaning "one who prevails with God" or "let God prevail," Israel received again the promises of the covenant. "And God said unto him, I am God Almighty: be fruitful and multiply; a nation and a company of nations shall be of thee, and kings shall come out of thy loins; and the land which I gave Abraham and Isaac, to thee I will give it, and to thy seed after thee will I give the land" (Genesis 35:11–12). And as before, Israel marked the holy site by pouring consecrated oil on a pillar (meaning altar) at the place and again calling it Beth-el, the house of God (Genesis 35:14–15).

The children of Abraham have since then been known simply as Israel.[74]

## The Covenant Renewed to the Next Generation

Israel was a patriarch to his sons, whom we now call "tribes." Israel called for two of his grandsons, Ephraim and Manasseh, who were born through Joseph. Israel then adopted Ephraim and Manasseh as his own sons. "And now thy two sons, Ephraim and Manasseh, which were born unto thee in the land of Egypt before I came unto thee into Egypt, are mine; as Reuben and Simeon, they shall be mine" (Genesis 48:5). This act of adoption illustrates the blessings of the covenant being passed down throughout the house of Israel.

Israel's choosing the sons of Joseph may be symbolic of one of the blessings of the Abrahamic covenant—being born of the Savior. We know Joseph to be one of the great scriptural types of the Savior. For example, both were shepherds (Genesis 37:2; John 10:11). Joseph and Jesus Christ were banished to Egypt, after efforts by Judah and Judas (*Judas* being the Latin form of *Judah*) to sell them for the price of a slave (Genesis 37:26–28; Matthew 2:13; 27:3). Both Joseph and Jesus were wrongfully imprisoned with two others (Genesis 40:2–3; Luke 23:32–33). Both became the means of salvation to those who had betrayed them (Genesis 45:7; Hebrews 5:9).

Understanding Joseph to be a scriptural type of Jesus Christ, this act of Israel adopting the sons of Joseph may symbolize the act of becoming sons and daughters of Christ through the Abrahamic covenant. Israel carried this covenant and bore the priesthood to administer it. Those who enter into the covenant and are faithful to it become the sons and daughters of Christ. In Genesis 48, the sons of Joseph—the symbolic sons of Jesus Christ—also become the sons of Israel.

## The Patriarchal Order Embodied

With Isaac, Jacob, Ephraim, and Manasseh, the blessings of the Abrahamic covenant were passed down from father to son. This follows the same patriarchal order of blessing the children of Adam, established from the beginning (D&C 107:40–41). This is the order of the priesthood and the blessings of the fathers that Abraham sought in the beginning (see Abraham 1).

In the case of Isaac, Jacob, Ephraim, and Manasseh, those blessings were promised through patriarchal blessings and later confirmed through temple experiences. This pattern remains unchanged with the Restoration of the gospel. In the restored gospel, patriarchal blessings give a priceless roadmap leading to the temple, where the blessings of the patriarchal order of the priesthood are found.

The story of Abraham, Isaac, and Jacob is by far the most complete example of this order that we have in the scriptures. In them, we see generations blessed. We see examples of an eternal family, of patriarchs presiding over their families in righteousness, and of patriarchs teaching and blessing their posterity so that they can receive the same blessings they received. Like God the Father, Abraham, Isaac, and Jacob were unfailing examples of righteous fathers whose sole objective was to bless their posterity and bring them the blessings of the fulness of the gospel. Having obtained their own assurance of an inheritance with God the Father, they wanted nothing more than to echo the words of Luke: "Son, thou art ever with me, and all that I have is thine" (Luke 15:31).

## *Who Is Israel?*

The story of Abraham, Isaac, and Jacob reveals clear and unmistakable scriptural types. In Genesis 22, we see Abraham—the "father of a multitude"—commanded to offer up his only begotten son. So in this instance, Abraham was an unmistakable symbol of God the Father.

In the same story, Isaac was about to be sacrificed. Only two people in all of scripture bear the title of "only begotten son." Isaac shared this title with Jesus Christ Himself (Hebrews 11:17; John 3:16). There is no indication in Genesis 22 or any other scripture that Isaac protested his father's actions. No doubt, he would've preferred to be spared from the sacrifice and have the cup pass from him, but he submitted anyway. The blessings of the covenant were secured by the Lord's oath as a result of Isaac's sacrifice, just as the Atonement—the sacrifice of the Only Begotten Son of God—secures all covenant blessings for us. Here, Isaac was a clear and unmistakable symbol of the Savior.

Consider also Hugh Nibley's teachings that link Abraham, Isaac, and Jacob as an inseparable trio. Nibley cited ancient traditions that compare Abraham to a morning prayer, Isaac to a noon prayer, and

Jacob to an evening prayer.[75] The scriptures don't give such a clear parallel for Jacob, but his place in Brother Nibley's prayer paradigm represents his symbolic identity. That identity is not taught through a scriptural experience like the *akedah* or binding in Genesis 22, but it is clear and extremely important to us.

The Father, represented by Abraham, came first, and then the Son, represented by Isaac, came in the middle of the day—the meridian of time. Jacob then came in the latter days.

Who is Jacob (or Israel) in both Brother Nibley's paradigm and scriptural symbolism?

We are.

We are modern Israel, the heirs to the covenant in the latter days. Christ, symbolized by Isaac, came in the meridian of time and gave life to Israel, represented by the evening or the latter days in Brother Nibley's model.

Isaac's victory over death, symbolized by being spared on Mount Moriah, gave way not just to the perpetuation of the covenant but to Israel himself.

All of the blessings of the fathers were passed down to Israel and Israel's posterity, represented by Ephraim and Manasseh. These blessings are not history or fable; they are the blessings available to every Latter-day Saint through the temple.

We are modern Israel, and the blessings of the Abrahamic covenant flow through us just as surely as they flowed through Isaac and Jacob anciently.

## The Gathering of Israel and the Family

One particular blessing of the Abrahamic covenant to modern Israel is the blessing of gathering. One of the most common references to Israel in our day is to the gathering of Israel. Jacob's sons each formed their own "tribe." Under the rule of King David, all of these tribes were unified as one glorious, all-powerful kingdom. After some time, the tribes fell apart, were captured by enemies, and were eventually scattered around the world. Israel remained scattered throughout the subsequent apostasies.

As part of the Restoration of the gospel, Israel is now being gathered all around the world. The heirs to the Abrahamic covenant are gathering as they receive the ordinances of baptism and the temple. All of the seed of Abraham, spread throughout the world, are now returning home to receive the blessings promised to Abraham anciently. Unhallowed hands of the world are trying to thwart the missionary and temple work that gathers Israel through the covenants and ordinances of the gospel, but it doesn't matter. The Lord has prophesied it. It is happening, and it will continue to happen until the work is finished.

In essence, the scattering of Israel was a splintering of the Lord's chosen family; the gathering of Israel is the reconciliation and coming home of the Lord's chosen family.

This gathering—this healing of a family—is a promised blessing not just for the world but also within our own families. It is also one of the most reassuring doctrines in the entire gospel when our children, like scattered Israel, stray from the covenant into which they were born.

Elder Orson F. Whitney taught,

> You parents of the wilful and the wayward! Don't give them up. Don't cast them off. They are not utterly lost. The Shepherd will find his sheep. They were his before they were yours—long before he entrusted them to your care; and you cannot begin to love them as he loves them. They have but strayed in ignorance from the Path of Right, and God is merciful to ignorance. Only the fulness of knowledge brings the fulness of accountability. Our Heavenly Father is far more merciful, infinitely more charitable, than even the best of his servants, and the Everlasting Gospel is mightier in power to save than our narrow finite minds can comprehend.
>
> The Prophet Joseph Smith declared—and he never taught more comforting doctrine—that the eternal sealings of faithful parents and the divine promises made to them for valiant service in the Cause of Truth, would save not only themselves, but likewise their posterity. Though some of the sheep may wander, the eye of the Shepherd is upon them, and sooner or later they will feel . . . Divine Providence reaching out after them and drawing them back to the fold. Either in this life or in the life to come, they will return. They will have to pay their debt to justice; they will suffer for their sins; and may tred a thorny path; but if it leads them at last, like the penitent Prodigal, to a loving and forgiving father's heart and home, the painful experience

> will not have been in vain. Pray for your careless and disobedient children; hold on to them with your faith. Hope on, trust on, till you see the salvation of God.[76]

More recently, President James E. Faust expounded in reference to Elder Whitney's teaching, "A principle in this statement that is often overlooked is that [children who have strayed from the covenant] must fully repent and 'suffer for their sins' and 'pay their debt to justice.' . . . The sealing power of faithful parents will only claim wayward children upon the condition of their repentance and Christ's Atonement."[77]

This doctrine is evident clear back to the days of Abraham and Isaac. When Isaac first received the promise of the covenant blessings, the Lord gave Isaac (and us) a simple but powerful lesson on why Isaac would be so blessed. "Because that Abraham obeyed my voice, and kept my charge, my commandments, my statutes, and my laws" (Genesis 26:5).

This is huge. Like Abraham, we have within our agency the ability to earn blessings for our posterity. Again, that is the goal of all the great patriarchs from Adam to Abraham to us. We want to bless our families and bring them back into the presence of God. Our own righteousness within the covenant carries that power, as taught by Elder Orson F. Whitney, President James E. Faust, and the Prophet Joseph Smith.

On a global scale, scattered Israel will be gathered because of the righteous builders of the kingdom. On a smaller scale within the family sealed in the temple, scattered Israel will be gathered through the faithfulness, prayers, and efforts of righteous parents.

- *The blessings of the Abrahamic covenant did not stop with Abraham.*
- *Rebekah, Isaac's wife, was actually the first person after Abraham and Sarah to receive the promised blessings of the covenant. The blessings were then reiterated to Isaac and eventually to his son Jacob.*
- *Abraham, Isaac, and Jacob received the promise of these blessings at different points throughout their lives. Sometimes, the blessings were promised through a patriarchal blessing. Other times, the blessings were received through temple experiences.*
- *Like Abraham's firstborn son, Ishmael, Isaac's firstborn son, Esau, lost his covenant blessings. Ishmael did not receive the covenant blessings*

*because Hagar's marriage was outside of the covenant. Esau lost his blessings in large part because he married outside of the covenant.*

- *On his way to take a wife within the covenant, Jacob had a particularly revealing temple experience in which he beheld a ladder ascending from earth to heaven, and angels ascending and descending on the ladder. The rungs on Jacob's ladder leading to heaven symbolize the covenants and ordinances of the temple. Like Abraham, Jacob received a new name as a result of one of his temple experiences.*
- *The blessings of the Abrahamic covenant being passed from Abraham to Isaac, from Isaac to Jacob, and from Jacob to Ephraim and Manasseh illustrates the patriarchal order of the priesthood.*
- *The story of Abraham, Isaac, and Jacob is the most complete illustration we have in the scriptures of the Lord's way of government and blessing His children.*
- *Jacob adopted Ephraim and Manasseh, his grandsons through Joseph. As Joseph was a representation of Jesus Christ, Jacob's adoption of Ephraim and Manasseh may have represented the blessing of the Abrahamic covenant, becoming a son or daughter of Christ.*
- *Abraham was a remarkable representation of God the Father, Isaac of the Son of God, and Jacob (Israel) of us. We are modern Israel.*
- *The house of Israel was united as one family under the rule of King David. Israel was later scattered throughout the world, representing the great apostasy.*
- *With the Restoration of the gospel, Israel is being gathered, and the heirs of the Abrahamic covenant are returning to the Lord's Church through the ordinances and covenants of baptism and the temple.*
- *The Lord has promised through modern-day prophets that righteous parents in the Abrahamic covenant will be blessed to have their own wayward children return to them if the parents are faithful in the covenant. This promise follows the same pattern of the gathering of Israel on a global scale.*

# Section Three

## The Works of Abraham

**W*ith an understanding*** of the blessings of the Abrahamic covenant, we will now learn what we need to do to receive those blessings. Doctrine and Covenants 132 reveals the account of the Prophet Joseph Smith receiving the greatest blessing that can be received in mortality—being sealed up unto eternal life, which is the culmination of the Abrahamic covenant, as we saw in Genesis 22. It is also the culmination of the temple experience. To Joseph, the Lord spoke, "For I am the Lord thy God, and will be with thee even unto the end of the world, and through all eternity; for verily I seal upon you your exaltation, and prepare a throne for you in the kingdom of my Father, with Abraham your father. Behold, I have seen your sacrifices, and will forgive all your sins; I have seen your sacrifices in obedience to that which I have told you. Go, therefore, and I make a way for your escape, as I accepted the offering of Abraham of his son Isaac" (D&C 132:49–50).

In the same section, the Lord taught that one receives this culmination of the blessings of Abraham, Isaac, and Jacob by doing "the works of Abraham" (D&C 132:32). As we have spent several chapters discussing the blessings of Abraham, we will now learn of the pattern set by Abraham to receive those blessings. There are four main chapters in Genesis where the Lord gave specific laws and instructions to Abraham in connection with the promises given. Each of these chapters teaches the laws needed to obtain the fulness of the covenant blessings.

In researching this subject, I was amazed at how many biblical scholars concluded that the blessings promised to Abraham were unilateral and unconditional from the beginning. Many learned people seem to believe that Abraham had to do absolutely nothing to receive the blessings promised to him. I don't understand the scriptural basis for this conclusion, as the Lord clearly gave Abraham many commandments, including most notably the commandment to offer Isaac as a sacrifice.

Satan has gotten great mileage by teaching people, "Eat, drink, and be merry; nevertheless, fear God—he will justify in committing a little sin; yea, lie a little, take the advantage of one because of his words, dig a pit for thy neighbor; there is no harm in this; and do all these things, for tomorrow we die; and if it so be that we are guilty, God will beat us with a few stripes, and at last we shall be saved in the kingdom of God" (2 Nephi 28:8).

This is an attractive doctrine to the world. Unfortunately, it is also a dangerous and even pernicious doctrine. In fact, it is a doctrine that destroys agency because it separates the two elements of agency: choice and accountability. Our choices, for good or bad, are worthless if they do not lead to accountability.

The Pearl of Great Price teaches that Lucifer was cast out because he sought to destroy agency (Moses 4:3). Many people view this scripture as meaning that he would somehow turn us into robots, with no choice. I personally believe that he sought to destroy agency not by removing choice but by removing accountability, just as taught in 2 Nephi 28:8. As I see it, he would offer blanket and unconditional forgiveness and make salvation unconditional, just as many view the Abrahamic covenant as being unconditional, with no faith, repentance, or ordinances needed.

It seems obvious to us that we would be saved by grace only "after all we can do" (2 Nephi 25:23). Still, there remain many in the Church who follow some degree or another this no-repentance philosophy when it comes to the blessings of the Abrahamic covenant. For example, I have heard far too many people speak of their spouses almost as property because they were "sealed" together. I have heard unrepentant adulterers boast of their "eternal" marriages and families.

It doesn't work that way. These people have received a celestial marriage ordinance but *live* a lower marriage in reality. These are stark examples, but they serve to remind us of the need for absolute fidelity to our covenants if we hope for the blessings promised through them. We have to see the bigger picture of our own responsibilities before we think of our eternal rights.

Paul taught of this or similar shortsightedness when he spoke, "For they are not all Israel, which are of Israel" (Romans 9:7). Paul further taught that even those within the covenant must still seek the law of righteousness by faith (see Romans 9:31–32).

As heirs to Abraham's blessings, we want to be counted as modern Israel. We want to be Abraham's children in every sense of the term. We enter into this covenant through the ordinances of the temple, and we must keep those covenants as Abraham did. Elder Stephen L. Richards said, "All the blessings of the temples are predicated upon faithfulness, upon obedience to the commandments. No blessing is effective unless it is based upon the good life of him who receives it."[78]

In a similar vein, President Spencer W. Kimball taught,

> All these ordinances are futile unless with them there is a great righteousness. . . . It is not enough to pay tithing and live the Word of Wisdom. We must be chaste in mind and in body. We must be neighborly, kind, and clean of heart. Sometimes people feel if they have complied with the more mechanical things that they are in line. And yet perhaps their hearts are not always pure. . . . With hearts that are absolutely purged and cleaned . . . we are prepared to come into the holy temple . . . where perfection should be found.[79]

Simply put, to receive the blessings of Abraham requires us to "do the works of Abraham," and this involves receiving and honoring the ordinances of the temple.

## The Abrahamic Covenant and the Fall

We have stated that Abraham and Sarah are role models, just like Adam and Eve, in their journey back to the presence of God. The works of Abraham illustrate this point, as they are the works that redeem us from the Fall.

Consider again Adam's condition before the Fall and compare that with the blessings promised to Abraham through his covenant. Adam was blessed with a land divinely prepared and granted, namely the Garden of Eden (Genesis 2:8). Abraham was promised Canaan. Adam was given dominion over all things in that land, and even the whole earth (Genesis 1:28). Abraham was promised the dominion of the priesthood. Adam was given free access to every tree in the Garden of Eden, including the tree of life, which represents the love of God, eternal life, and the presence of God (Genesis 2:16–17; 1 Nephi 11:25; Revelation 22:14). Abraham was promised eternal life in the presence of God. Adam was given his eternal companion, Eve (Genesis 2:18, 21–25). Together, they were commanded to multiply and replenish the earth (Genesis 1:28). Abraham was given Sarah, and they were promised that their seed would fill the earth and the heavens. With the Fall, Adam and Eve were cast out of Eden and were lost, completely dependent on a Savior to regain their eternal Eden. The Atonement is Christ's vicarious act for Adam and Eve and their posterity that reverses the effects of the Fall. The Abrahamic covenant is the coming together of man and God that puts the Atonement into full effect.

The pattern appears like this, in chiastic form:

- *Eden* (before the Fall)—blessings of the presence of God, property, priesthood, and posterity.
    - *The Fall*—Adam and Eve driven out of Eden and dependent on a Savior to regain Eden.
- *Abrahamic covenant* (redemption from the Fall)—the presence of God, priesthood, and posterity restored for eternity.

The parallels are unmistakable. The Abrahamic covenant, just like the Atonement, serves to reverse the effects of the Fall. The blessings of the Abrahamic covenant restore the condition that Adam and Eve enjoyed in the Garden of Eden.

This is neither a coincidence nor a mistake. Just as the blessings of the Abrahamic covenant are the blessings of the Atonement that reverse the Fall, the works of Abraham are the works that we must do within the covenant to take full advantage of the Atonement and reverse the effects of the Fall in our own lives.

# *Genesis 12*

## *"Get Thee . . . unto a Land That I Will Shew Thee"*

**G*enesis 12 begins*** with a straightforward commandment from the Lord to Abraham. "Get thee out of thy country, and from thy kindred, and from thy father's house, unto a land that I will shew thee" (Genesis 12:1). This is known in biblical circles as "the call." Following "the call," the Lord gave the first iteration of the blessings promised to Abraham. Consistent with the Lord's eternal order, the commandment always comes before the blessing, and Abraham's first experience was no exception (see Doctrine and Covenants 130:20–21). The Lord commanded, and he obeyed. "So [Abraham] departed, as the Lord had spoken unto him" (Genesis 12:4).

### *Obedience*

The law taught in this step of the covenant is obedience. The Lord was asking Abraham to leave behind his country, neighbors, and family and follow Him to an unspecified and unknown place. This invitation prefigures the Savior's familiar and timeless invitation to all of us, "Follow me."[80] Just as the Savior began His ministry by inviting the disciples to follow Him, the Abrahamic covenant began with the law of obedience.

Likewise, this commandment hearkens back to Abraham's foreordination in the premortal existence, where this great law of obedience was set as the first law of heaven. "And we will prove them herewith, to see if they will do all things whatsoever the Lord their God shall command them" (Abraham 3:25).

Obedience has been called the first law of heaven.[81] It is the foundation for every commandment and blessing from heaven. The Abrahamic covenant and the journey from the Fall back to the presence of God began with this divine law. This law necessarily has to come first because all blessings are predicated on obedience to commandments (see Doctrine and Covenants 130:20–21). Abraham's action in heeding the Lord's call embodies the Prophet Joseph Smith's motto: "I made this my rule: When God commands, do it!"[82]

## *Faith*

Closely linked—if not inseparably connected—with the law of obedience is the principle of faith. Just as obedience is the first law of heaven, faith in the Lord Jesus Christ is the first principle of the gospel (see Articles of Faith 1:4). Quite simply, obedience requires faith. Abraham is revered by Muslims, Jews, and Christians alike for the great faith he demonstrated in immediately heeding the call of the Lord to get up and move. This was the first of several examples of Abraham's great faith.

Abraham's example isn't easy for us to follow. Pack up. Take your family with you. Leave your land. Leave your father. Go somewhere. You don't know where yet, but go anyway. And go now. Truly, that was faith. That was devotion. That was obedience.

That is why faith in Jesus Christ—the Giver of the law that we follow, the Redeemer who bears the burden of our sins committed on the journey—is the first principle of the gospel, to guide us on our journey back to the presence of God.

## Obedience and Overcoming the Fall

Obedience serves as the condition for the Lord bestowing on us blessings. This is not its only purpose; the Lord wants us to become like Him. That requires not just purity from sin but also learning His ways. The law of obedience also serves to educate us to become more like God, to nurture our divine nature. In addressing BYU graduates, famed Hollywood director Cecil B. DeMille chose to speak to his Christian audience on the subject of obedience to God's commandments. Mr. DeMille, who directed perhaps the greatest epic on the subject of divine law, taught,

> We are too inclined to think of law as something merely restrictive—something hemming us in. We sometimes think of law as the opposite of liberty. But that is a false conception. That is not the way that God's inspired prophets and lawgivers looked upon the law. Law has a twofold purpose. It is meant to govern and it is also meant to educate. . . .
>
> And so it is with all the commandments.
>
> We must look beneath the literal, the surface meaning of the words. We must take the trouble to understand them; for how can we obey commands that we do not understand? But the commandments too have an educative function—which you can see in the life of anyone who keeps them. They produce good character. The Ten Commandments are not rules to obey as a personal favor to God. They are the fundamental principles without which mankind cannot live together. They make of those who keep them faithful, strong, wholesome, confident, dedicated men and women. This is so because the commandments come from the same Divine Hand that fashioned our human nature.
>
> God does not contradict Himself. He did not create man and then, as an afterthought, impose upon him a set of arbitrary, irritating, restrictive rules. He made man free—and then gave him the commandments to keep him free.[83]

The Lord designed obedience as the guiding principle throughout Abraham's journey back to His presence. This law was designed not just to guide Abraham through mortality but also to teach him how to be like God. This was a lifelong process for Abraham that culminated over the course of decades. It was not a one-shot deal where obeying one of the Lord's calls earned the fulness of the promised blessings. Remember, this was only Genesis 12. Genesis 22 was still decades of service, trials, and obedience away. Abraham did not receive the oath of the Lord for the promised blessings until he was tried many times in many different ways on many more occasions.

On our own journeys from whatever land the Lord has called us out of and through whatever trials may await, the law of obedience should be our constant guide. Whenever the Lord commands anything of us, our motto should be like Abraham's and Joseph Smith's: do it.

- *Before the Lord first gave great promises to Abraham, He commanded Abraham to get up and leave his country, friends, and father and follow the Lord to a new home. As soon as the Lord commanded, Abraham obeyed. This is a lesson on the law of obedience—the first law of heaven.*
- *Closely related to the law of obedience is the principle of faith. Abraham's willingness to leave his home and father demonstrated great faith, particularly as the Lord didn't even tell Abraham where He was taking him.*
- *Faith in the Lord Jesus Christ is the first principle of the gospel. Faith enables us to keep the Lord's commandments.*
- *The law of obedience teaches us to be like God. This is the purpose of the Atonement.*
- *Obedience is a guiding law throughout our lives. It is not a one-shot process where we can expect to receive all of the blessings of the covenant from one act alone. We still must be tried and proven like Abraham before we can hope to receive the eternal blessings of the Abrahamic covenant.*

# Genesis 15

## Sacrifice and "Cutting" Covenant

**Following Genesis 12,** Genesis 15 is the next great and comprehensive promise of the blessings of the Abrahamic covenant. Like the Lord's invitation in Genesis 12 to obey His voice, the Lord also followed the promise of blessings in Genesis 15 with a law—the law of sacrifice.

> After these things the word of the Lord came unto [Abraham] in a vision, saying, Fear not, [Abraham]: I am thy shield, and thy exceeding great reward.
>
> And [Abraham] said, Lord God, what wilt thou give me, seeing I go childless, and the steward of my house is this Eliezer of Damascus?
>
> And [Abraham] said, Behold, to me thou hast given no seed: and, lo, one born in my house is mine heir.
>
> And, behold, the word of the Lord came unto him, saying, This shall not be thine heir; but he that shall come forth out of thine own bowels shall be thine heir.
>
> And he brought him forth abroad, and said, Look now toward heaven, and tell the stars, if thou be able to number them: and he said unto him, So shall thy seed be.
>
> And he believed in the Lord; and he counted it to him for righteousness.

> And he said unto him, I am the Lord that brought thee out of Ur of the Chaldees, to give thee this land to inherit it.
>
> And he said, Lord God, whereby shall I know that I shall inherit it?
>
> And he said unto him, Take me an heifer of three years old, and a she goat of three years old, and a ram of three years old, and a turtledove, and a young pigeon.
>
> And he took unto him all these, and divided them in the midst, and laid each piece one against another: but the birds divided he not. (Genesis 15:1–10)

The Lord teaches great lessons through the symbolism of Genesis 15. As with the symbolism in the temple, this is a subject matter we have to reach deeper to understand.

So let's reach deeper.

## The Law of Sacrifice

Following Abraham's second question in this exchange, the Lord directed Abraham to take animals, sacrifice them, and lay them together (Genesis 15:9). The requirement that the sacrificial animals be three years old was likely a prefiguring of the Savior, who would be offered as a sacrifice at the age of thirty-three.

With no further question, Abraham promptly complied (Genesis 15:10). This is the law of sacrifice.

With the first complete iteration of the blessings, the Lord taught Abraham the law of obedience and the principle of faith. Now, with the second complete iteration of the blessings, the Lord taught Abraham the law of sacrifice. Within the pattern of essential components of biblical covenant, the animals represented the sacrifice of the covenant and the blood of the covenant.

## The Principle of Repentance

Just as the law of obedience given to Abraham in Genesis 12 taught the principle of faith, the law of sacrifice is a scriptural lesson on the principle of repentance. The word *sacrifice* means to "make holy or sacred." Animal sacrifices were always a symbol of the sacrifice of the

Lamb of God, and this great and last sacrifice serves to atone for our sins and make repentance possible (see Alma 17:10–17). Obedience leads to sacrifice in the same way that faith leads to repentance.

An angel of the Lord taught this same lesson to Adam when he offered animal sacrifices after he and Eve were expelled from the Garden of Eden.

> And after many days an angel of the Lord appeared unto Adam, saying: Why dost thou offer sacrifices unto the Lord? And Adam said unto him: I know not, save the Lord commanded me.
>
> And then the angel spake, saying: This thing is a similitude of the sacrifice of the Only Begotten of the Father, which is full of grace and truth.
>
> Wherefore, thou shalt do all that thou doest in the name of the Son, and thou shalt *repent* and call upon God in the name of the Son forevermore. (Moses 5:6–8; emphasis added)

We are not asked to sacrifice animals in the latter days. Instead, we offer a broken—or willing—heart and a contrite—or changed—spirit (3 Nephi 9:19–20). These are the hallmarks of repentance that lead to a new, spiritual birth.

## "Cutting" Covenant

Abraham literally cutting the heifer, goat, and ram in half is foreign or perhaps flat-out strange to most people. Some of that mystery is lifted with a little more understanding of the language barrier. In addition to being a sacrifice, this act was also a reference to covenants and ordinances. In English, we say that we *make* or *enter into* a covenant. In biblical Hebrew, Abraham would have *cut* a covenant. The Hebrew verb that accompanies the Hebrew noun for covenant (*berith*) is *karat*, which means literally "to cut." So, while we *make* or *enter into* a covenant, Abraham would have *cut* a covenant.

This practice is a "ritual of covenant making, which in a similar form, was well known to many ancient peoples."[84] We would refer to this as an ordinance.

Genesis 15 doesn't explicitly state that Abraham passed through the pieces of the sacrificed animals, but it is implied from our understanding of the ancient practice.

While the animals were the sacrifice of the covenant, the ritual of cutting the animals in this manner and passing through them constituted the seal or token or sign of the covenant. Under the system of biblical covenants, these rituals, ordinances, seals, signs, or tokens of the covenant were the "tangible witness," or physical proof, of the covenant. When Abraham asked, "Whereby shall I know that I shall inherit it?" he was not expressing doubt (Genesis 15:8). To the contrary, he was asking for a tangible witness or physical proof of the covenant. He was asking for an ordinance, seal, sign, or token of the covenant.

This ritual (as in, this ordinance) of "cutting" covenants is not as foreign to us as it may appear. We were born into this world because of the premortal covenant we made to accept Jesus and follow Heavenly Father's plan. In the act of birth, we cut or passed through a veil. In the covenant of baptism, we cut or pass through the waters of baptism. As we live that covenant and endure to the end, we pass through many trials that are part of the mortality experience. Ultimately, we hope to cut or pass back through the veil and return to our Heavenly Father (see Matthew 27:51). With the help of the Holy Ghost, all of us can learn to recognize other gospel ordinances or seals of covenants that invoke this imagery of "cutting."

The Lord required Abraham to sacrifice and cut in half three different animals as part of this ritual, or ordinance. This invokes images of the three degrees of glory. This ordinance of the Abrahamic covenant involves ascending through the telestial, terrestrial, and celestial kingdoms, just as Abraham's grandson Jacob would experience when the Lord gave him the vision of the ladder with its three main rounds.[85] As a partner to this covenant and a participant in the ordinance, Abraham would have walked through the carcasses of three animals, each representing a kingdom of glory, just like the ladder his grandson Jacob would see in a vision.

## The Cursing of a Covenant Broken

In true Old Testament fashion, this practice also served as a reminder of the fate awaiting those who break their covenants. Some 1,400 years later, the book of Jeremiah referred to the same practice of cutting a sacrificial animal as a means of expressing a covenant. However, this time, the practice also illustrated the curse of breaking a covenant rather than the blessings of keeping the covenant.

> Therefore thus saith the Lord; Ye have not hearkened unto me . . . and I will make you to be removed into all the kingdoms of the earth.
>
> And I will give the men that have transgressed my covenant, which have not performed the words of the covenant which they had made before me, when they cut the calf in twain, and passed between the parts thereof,
>
> The princes of Judah, and the princes of Jerusalem, the eunuchs, and the priests, and all the people of the land, which passed between the parts of the calf. (Jeremiah 34:17–19)

The imagery of a slain animal cut in two served both as a lesson on the great and last sacrifice—the Atonement—and on the dismembered fate of those who break their covenants.

## The Opposition to Sacred Covenants and Ordinances

Using another layer of symbolism, Genesis 15 also teaches of the adversary's opposition to the covenant. "And when the fowls came down upon the carcases, Abram drove them away. And when the sun was going down, a deep sleep fell upon Abram; and, lo, an horror of great darkness fell upon him" (Genesis 15:11–12). The footnote for this scripture leads to Joseph Smith—History 1:15–17, which is the account of the First Vision where Satan tried to intervene and stop a sacred experience. E. Douglas Clark cited ancient extra-biblical sources further describing this interruption as a demonic attempt to keep Abraham from concluding the act. One source, the Apocalypse of Abraham, stated that one of the birds that swooped down on the sacrifices was Satan himself.[86] According to this, Abraham was comforted and protected by an angel who intervened at the ominous occasion. This same source named this angel as Abraham's role model, Enoch.[87]

This event prefigured the opposition that the adversary sends to thwart us from getting to the temple. Whether we're going through the preparation process or trying to get out the door, it is amazing what curveballs the adversary makes up to keep us from the sacred experiences found there.

When they hit, think of Abraham. Remember that you're facing the same opposition that he faced. Recognize the source of that opposition, and then beat it. Sometimes that may come up with the help of a messenger sent by the Lord, or sometimes you'll just have to shoo away that bird all on your own. But you can do it.

## Because He Asked

It is worth noting that the Lord reiterated the blessings of the covenant to Abraham simply because Abraham asked. Abraham first asked, "What wilt thou give me, seeing I go childless" (Genesis 15:2). This was Abraham's prayer. No doubt, it was a much more direct prayer than you and I would typically offer, but it was a prayer nonetheless, and the kind of prayer that you and I should strive to offer. The Lord spoke to Abraham, and Abraham spoke right back, seeking direction from the Lord.

If this plea for direction seems like a complaint or a lack of faith for the blessings previously promised to Abraham, consider: "And he believed in the Lord; and he counted it to him for righteousness" (Genesis 15:6). Abraham's faith did not waiver, and the apparent questioning of the blessing of posterity promised earlier but still not received was not a complaint. This is a lesson to us not to counsel the Lord, but to continually ask in faith where we stand before Him.

After the Lord reiterated the blessing of the promised land, Abraham asked, "And he said, Lord God, whereby shall I know that I shall inherit it?" (Genesis 15:8). Abraham again asked for what he needed to do or needed to know, and the Lord taught him something new. As we saw previously, the Lord gave him the seal, or sign, of the covenant.

- *In Genesis 15, the Lord gave Abraham the full promises of the covenant a second time and accompanied this second promise with a commandment to offer sacrifices.*
- *This law of sacrifice builds on the law of obedience given to Abraham in Genesis 12 and is a parallel to the principle of repentance.*

*Sacrifices were offered in similitude of the Savior's Atonement, which makes repentance possible.*

- *The particular form of sacrifice directed by the Lord is an Old Testament ritual that accompanies a covenant. This is a parallel to the ordinances that accompany covenants of the gospel.*
- *In the Hebrew language of the Old Testament account, one would* cut *a covenant, whereas in English we would say that one* makes *or* enters into *a covenant.*
- *This reference to "cutting" a covenant is a lesson on several ordinances that are more familiar to us. The act of "cutting" a covenant is a seal, or sign or token, of the Abrahamic covenant.*
- *Abraham overcame an ominous experience, much like Joseph Smith in the sacred grove, as part of this experience. This is a lesson to us to recognize and overcome the opposition that often precedes temple visits.*
- *Abraham received the instruction of Genesis 15 in large part because he asked.*

# Genesis 17, Part One

## "Walk before Me, and Be Thou Perfect"

In ***Genesis 17,*** the Lord gave Abraham the full promises of the covenant for the third time. Before this promise, the chapter began with the Lord giving Abraham another law to live. "I am the Almighty God; walk before me, and be thou perfect" (Genesis 17:1).

Other translations of the Bible render this passage, "Walk with me and be blameless" (New International Version), "Walk in my ways and be blameless" (Alter Translation), and "Live in my presence, be perfect" (Wenham and Vawter).[88] These alternate translations accurately reflect the symbolic meaning of walking before God and the quest to become perfect.

## Not One Solitary Law, But a Way of Life

Generally speaking, walking represents the way we live our everyday lives. To walk with or before God or in His presence is to live a holy and upright life. The entry for "walk" in the Topical Guide in the scriptures links to other subjects such as "behave" and "live." Think of it—each day of life, we walk thousands of steps. These steps combine to forge a path. This path is the way we live. Walking before God means taking thousands of steps each day in the path of holiness and righteousness.

The laws given to Abraham in Genesis 12 and 15 were succinctly demarcated in contrast to this law. Here, the Lord was asking Abraham not just to live one law, but to walk before God—to live his entire life in the path that leads to perfection. That meant asking Abraham to live his life according to *every* law and word that proceeded forth from the mouth of God (Matthew 4:4).

Walking before God was also given as an umbrella of gospel laws in the Doctrine and Covenants. "And this shall be our covenant—that we will walk in all the ordinances of the Lord" (D&C 136:4). In this sense, walking represents obedience to all of the ordinances (and laws and covenants that accompany them) that lead to the ultimate goal of Zion.

Also in the Doctrine and Covenants, the promises of the Word of Wisdom were specifically linked to walking before God by obeying the commandments—plural. "And all saints who remember to keep and do these sayings, *walking in obedience to the commandments*, shall receive health in their navel and marrow to their bones; and shall find wisdom and great treasures of knowledge, even hidden treasures; and shall run and not be weary, and shall *walk* and not faint" (D&C 89:18–20; emphasis added). Obedience to the Word of Wisdom brings a promise that we will not faint as we, like Abraham, walk before God in obedience to the commandments given and the covenants we have made.

Having walked before God, our lives will serve as testament of laws obeyed and covenants kept. That is the goal of walking before God, as Abraham was instructed. Elder Bruce R. McConkie taught, "In the final analysis, the gospel of God is written, not in the dead letters of scriptural records, but in the lives of the Saints. It is not written with pen and ink on paper of man's making, but with acts and deeds in the book of life of each believing and obedient person. It is engraved in the flesh and bones and sinews of those who live a celestial law, which is the law of the gospel."[89]

Elder McConkie's term *the law of the gospel* is a fitting title to the law given to Abraham in Genesis 17 that he walk before God and become perfect. Elder William R. Bradford spoke on this subject in the October 1977 general conference, teaching that this law is so vast and broad that we must study the scriptures to learn its entirety. He likewise said that this law encompasses service to one another, tithes and offerings, honesty, and "the many laws that together comprise the law of the gospel."[90]

Elder Bradford summarized this law by citing the conclusion of the Book of Mormon, which contains this law. Not surprisingly, this scripture contains Abrahamic covenant references that you will likely recognize.

> And again I would exhort you that ye would come unto Christ, and lay hold upon every good gift, and touch not the evil gift, nor the unclean thing.
>
> And awake, and arise from the dust, O Jerusalem; yea, and put on thy beautiful garments, O daughter of Zion; and strengthen thy stakes and enlarge thy borders forever, that thou mayest no more be confounded, that the covenants of the Eternal Father which he hath made unto thee, O house of Israel, may be fulfilled.
>
> Yea, come unto Christ, and be perfected in him, and deny yourselves of all ungodliness; and if ye shall deny yourselves of all ungodliness, and love God with all your might, mind and strength, then is his grace sufficient for you, that by his grace ye may be perfect in Christ; and if by the grace of God ye are perfect in Christ, ye can in nowise deny the power of God.
>
> And again, if ye by the grace of God are perfect in Christ, and deny not his power, then are ye sanctified in Christ by the grace of God, through the shedding of the blood of Christ, which is in the covenant of the Father unto the remission of your sins, that ye become holy, without spot. (Moroni 10:30–33)

This law of the gospel—to walk before God—also leads to the ultimate goal of being perfect, as taught by Moroni and referenced by Elder Bradford. As shown in other translations, this word could also be translated as "blameless" or even "complete." Moroni then concluded the Book of Mormon with this invitation to us to become blameless and complete—and therefore perfect—by putting the Atonement into full practice. Such a level of holiness in and through Christ is the product of walking before God. This end is the culmination of the

Savior's teaching in the Sermon on the Mount and at the temple to the Nephites. "Therefore I would that ye should be perfect even as I, or your Father who is in heaven is perfect" (3 Nephi 12:48; see also Matthew 5:48).

Here it is also important to understand that being "perfect" in a biblical sense means to keep one's covenants.[91] As the law of the gospel comprises multiple laws under one covenant umbrella, this is the commandment to become like God. This commandment is epitomized in the transition from being Adam (meaning "mankind") to becoming Michael (meaning "who is like God"). Adam's progression, signified by his new name, followed this path from mortality to immortality, from weakness to perfection, from corruption to incorruption. The Abrahamic covenant is the means for us to follow this same progression and receive all that the Father hath (D&C 84:38).

In other words, the law of the gospel given to Abraham was the path for Abraham to follow the rest of his life. Abraham was being taught to enter into this way and endure to the end in it until he became perfect, like God, through faithfulness to his covenants.

Brigham Young chose the same word *walk* to teach of the temple endowment and all of the ordinances received therein. "Your endowment is, to receive all those ordinances in the House of the Lord, which are necessary for you, after you have departed this life, *to enable you to walk back to the presence of the Father*, passing the angels who stand as sentinels, being enabled to give them the key words, the signs and tokens pertaining to the Holy Priesthood, and gain your eternal exaltation in spite of earth and hell."[92] Here again, walking represents the sum of our lives' works as received in the temple—the ordinances, covenants, and laws received in the temple and honored throughout our lives. If we are faithful to each of them, then the ultimate blessing is to be able to finish the walk back to the presence of the Father.

The collective ordinances comprising the endowment therefore represent the ultimate act of walking not just *before* God but also *back* to God.

## A Possible Parallel with the Ordinance of Baptism

The law of obedience given in Genesis 12 is linked with the principle of faith, and the law of sacrifice given in Genesis 15 is linked with the principle of repentance. In Genesis 17, Abraham was asked to live his life before God, abandoning anything that wasn't in harmony with His teachings. In that sense, Genesis 17 may parallel the ordinance of baptism, which leads to a whole new life where the former self is symbolically buried (Romans 6:4), and a spiritually reborn person emerges (John 3:5). Baptism leads to a new life as a living disciple of Christ, or one who walks before God.

## A Personal Observation on Walking

The Savior taught that the "light of the body is the eye: if therefore thine eye be single, thy whole body shall be full of light. But if thine eye be evil, thy whole body shall be full of darkness. If therefore the light that is in thee be darkness, how great is that darkness" (Matthew 6:22–23). There is a real and direct link between the eyes and the feet. Our feet follow our eyes, for good or bad.

Several years ago, our family participated in a challenge course activity. A tight rope was set up ten or fifteen feet above the ground, and we had the thrill of walking it—with the aid of many safety precautions, of course. I think I was the first one in the family to give it a try, so naturally I had to be tough and march right through it like a brave guy. I started slowly, watching my feet every inch to be sure that they were square on the tightrope. After a few short, unimpressive, and—well—wobbly strides, the lady at the other end of the tightrope held out her hand to me. She said simply, "Don't look at your feet. Look at me. Reach for my hand."

It really was as simple as that. Immediately, my path straightened, and I stopped wobbling. I finished the last 90 percent of the way over the tightrope in less time than the first 10 percent had taken me.

My feet instinctively followed my eyes. My path seemed to straighten itself as I focused on the destination. The path to that destination took care of itself.

Several years later, I took up a challenge from two dear friends, Rob and Lori, to run a marathon. That was no easy task. At times, I wanted to find and slug whoever decided that running 26.2 miles was the ultimate test of human endurance. But it was infinitely worth it, and that experience gave me so much to be grateful for and carried me through the upcoming trials in my life.

In training for that marathon, I learned some pretty painful things about running. I learned that landing on my heel when I ran was not a good thing. For one, I was wearing through shoes way too quickly. I also learned that this stride pattern slowed me down, like hitting the brakes with each stride. Finally, I learned that running this way was likely to take its toll on my joints and lead me to an injury that would keep me from finishing the race and meeting this suddenly critical goal I had set.

I researched the subject and did everything I could think of to end my heel-striking problem and learn to land on the middle of my feet. Nothing seemed to help. I was still wearing through shoes like butter, and my stride didn't feel fluid. Well, I got through that first marathon, and I ended up with one of the worst cases of *plantar fasciitis*—a most painful and annoying foot condition—that my doctor and physical therapist had ever seen. But by then, I was officially hooked. I just had to keep running.

Finally, after too many pairs of shoes and more foot pain than I could quantify, I found a solution. As with the tightrope, the solution was not in my feet, but in my eyes. I found that, if I kept my eyes fixated thirty to forty feet in front of me, something magical happened. My whole body aligned. My stride carried me naturally to a mid-foot strike, not the painful heel strike.

And that was only the beginning of the benefits. You see, when you get tired on long runs, you tend to stare down at the ground. With your eyes staring down, you slow down and tend to miss things in your path—things like rocks, curbs, dogs, and the occasional, uh, car. Those things can ruin a good run pretty quickly. When your eyes are focused in front of you thirty or forty feet, you see the little things and the big things too. You see the whole picture, which you need to stay safe and to keep going. Your feet carry you safely.

And so, yet again, I learned the magical lesson that your feet follow your eyes.

What are we feeding our eyes? Are we placing before them the scriptures or trash? Are we using them to seek for eternal treasure or for quick, carnal pleasure? Are they fixed on moment or on the eternal goal?

As you contemplate walking before the Lord toward perfection and blamelessness, remember this simple but oh-so-helpful lesson. My friends—especially the brethren—your feet follow your eyes.

## *A Personal Lesson on Walking and the Covenant of the Priesthood*

Several years ago, my father called me late at night to tell me that my sister Shauna had been in a terrible car crash. My nieces, Stephanie and Amanda, were in the car also, but they were somehow fine. My sister, however, suffered multiple traumatic injuries.

When we arrived at the hospital, we learned more about the accident. A driver in a rented minivan had run a red light and hit my sister right on her door at full speed. The impact was so violent that the driver of the minivan had been thrown out from one of the rear windows and landed about eighty feet from the point of impact. He had been killed instantly. My sister had already received a miracle just by surviving the crash.

But there in the emergency room, she lay in need of another miracle. This was her greatest hour of need, and the Lord had sent His priesthood holders—my father, my brother, Scott, and me—to work another miracle through a priesthood blessing. The three of us laid our hands on her head, and my brother pronounced a beautiful blessing that I will never forget. My sister received that additional miracle. She lives and walks today through the Lord's blessing, administered by His priesthood.

That moment surrounding her hospital bed with my father and brother was perhaps the proudest moment of my life. There was my sister, frankly and fully in need of a miracle, and there were three worthy priesthood holders in a position to call down those blessings from heaven. She was in need, and we were worthy to address that need. The experience reminded me of one of my favorite stories I'd read years before from Elder Vaughn J. Featherstone. He told the story of a farmer whose child had been electrocuted. The farmer took the child in his arms and by the authority of the Melchizedek Priesthood commanded the child to live. By the power of that priesthood, the child lived. Elder Featherstone then taught, "This great brother could not have possibly done that had he been looking at a pornographic piece of material a few nights before or if he had been involved in any other transgression of that kind."[93] The point was startlingly clear: the priesthood needs a pure conduit to work.

As if my sister's experience had not been enough, my wife, Cami, went into premature labor barely a week later. This was not good. Our last daughter, Kayla, had been born premature and had to be hooked up to a monitor for her first eight months of life because of the complications. That was a long and difficult experience that made us all too familiar with the perils of premature birth. So once again, my father came to the hospital late at night to give a blessing when we sorely needed divine intervention. After thirty-one hours of labor, it stopped. This blessing was fulfilled through a doctor, who also happened to be a worthy priesthood holder and felt inspired to administer an antibiotic along with the IV medication designed to stop the labor. As it turned out, the premature labor was caused by an infection. The medication designed to stop the contractions and labor did nothing, but the antibiotic eventually stopped the infection and labor. Claire was given a few more weeks to grow, and that made all the difference.

Brethren, we don't know when we will be called on to exercise the priesthood. We don't get advance notice about when someone even in our own family will depend on us to exercise that priesthood to call down a miracle from heaven. For the rest of my life, I will be grateful that I was worthy to be a part of that process when my family needed those miracles. I will always be thankful that my father and brother were able to step up in the moment of need and be that pure conduit for the powers of heaven. If any of us had taken even a day off from the priesthood we held and the laws that govern it, we would have regretted it forever, and our beloved family might have been left to pay the price.

That is a huge part of what it means to be "faithful unto the obtaining these two priesthoods" (D&C 84:33). To me, the faithfulness that underlies the oath and covenant of the priesthood is a function of walking before God. We demonstrate our faithfulness by the way we live each day of our lives. If we dare take a day off by giving in to temptation, we disqualify ourselves from being the pure conduit through whom the priesthood can function. "That [the rights of the priesthood] may be conferred upon us, it is true; but when we undertake to cover our sins, or to gratify our pride, our vain ambition, or to exercise control or dominion or compulsion upon the souls of the children of men, *in any degree of unrighteousness*, behold, the heavens withdraw themselves; the Spirit of the Lord is grieved; and when it is withdrawn, Amen to the priesthood or the authority of that man" (D&C 121:37; emphasis added).

It's just not worth the risk of letting our guard down. We honor the priesthood—we fulfill our part of the oath and covenant—by walking before God and living each day worthy to call down all the magnificent blessings that are available through the marvelous and eternal priesthood of God.

- *In Genesis 17, the Lord promised Abraham the blessings of the covenant for the third time. Before repeating the promises, the Lord gives Abraham a third law to live—to walk before Him and be perfect.*
- *Walking symbolizes the way we live our lives.*
- *In giving this law, the Lord was actually giving Abraham a whole set of gospel laws designed to govern the way Abraham lived his daily life.*
- *This collection of laws to govern the way we live our everyday lives has been called the law of the gospel. In some ways, this law is a parallel to the ordinance of baptism in that it represents a new life, walking in obedience to all the commandments of God.*
- *Following this law and living our lives in obedience to all the commandments of God leads to perfection through the Atonement of Jesus Christ.*
- *Generally speaking, our feet—that is, our walking before God—follow our eyes. If our eyes are fixed on the things of God, our feet will follow.*

# Genesis 17, Part Two

## "And It Shall Be a Token of the Covenant betwixt Me and You"

**In addition to** promising Abraham the complete blessings of the covenant for the third time, the Lord also changed Abraham's and Sarah's names in Genesis 17. This blessing of a new name that reflected the blessings promised to Abraham and Sarah was preceded by another commandment—another of the works of Abraham—which the Lord called "a token of the covenant." "This is my covenant, which ye shall keep, between me and you and thy seed after thee; every man child among you shall be circumcised. And ye shall circumcise the flesh of your foreskin; and it shall be a token of the covenant betwixt me and you" (Genesis 17:10–11).

Abraham then took himself, Ishmael, "all that were born in his house," and every male in his house to be circumcised "the selfsame day" (Genesis 17:23).

From that time, male children born into the covenant were circumcised at eight days old (Genesis 17:12). The Joseph Smith Translation of this passage serves as the latter-day teaching on the age of accountability and the instruction to baptize children when they reach eight years old, following the pattern established by circumcision at eight days (JST Genesis 17:11–12).

Put aside the awkwardness of the subject for a minute. There are great symbolic lessons on the covenant to be had here. First, the Lord called circumcision a "token of the covenant" (Genesis 17:11). This token was, again, the physical proof of the covenant. According to the *Encyclopedia of Mormonism*, the word *token* derives from the Greek word *sumbulon* (also the root of the word *symbol*), which literally means "to throw together."

That definition makes little sense until the context and application of the word are understood. The application of the word is an ancient practice used to formalize an agreement. "Contracting parties would break a *sumbolon,* a bone or a tally stick, into two pieces, then fit them together again later. Each piece would represent its owner; the halves 'thrown together' represent two separate identities merged into one."[94] Each party's token, or more specifically each party's part of the token, would be "thrown together" to fit with the other party's. The two halves then formed a single proof of the agreement—a single token. This concept of a token carries a unique significance in circumcision, as we will see shortly.

Second, the act of circumcision sheds blood and therefore serves as the blood of the covenant. Sacred covenants were and are life-and-death situations. The shedding of blood symbolically represented this life-and-death nature of the covenant and served as a foreshadowing of the blood of Jesus Christ. The cutting of the flesh likewise mirrored the concept of "cutting" covenant, as revealed in Genesis 15, as well as the fate of being "cut" off from the presence of the Lord, for those who break the covenant. "And the uncircumcised man child whose flesh of his foreskin is not circumcised, that soul shall be cut off from his people; he hath broken my covenant" (Genesis 17:14).

Third, this token was obviously a reference to seed and the blessing of posterity, both earthly and eternally. The token and commandment of circumcision were introduced not just for Abraham but also for his seed (Genesis 17:9–10, 12–13). The Abrahamic covenant and the patriarchal order of the priesthood that administers it are all about posterity. The patriarchal order of the priesthood specifically exists, according to Joseph Smith, to bring a patriarch's posterity back into the presence of God.[95]

## Chastity and the Marriage Covenant

Understanding that circumcision was a reference to posterity, it becomes clear that the token also implied the marriage covenant. In God's plan, children are entitled to be born within the bounds of marriage. Each time a couple kneels across the altar in a temple and is sealed under the authority of the priesthood, a new family in the Abrahamic covenant is created. "When sweethearts kneel at the temple altar and are joined by the power of the holy priesthood for time and all eternity, an eternal family is organized and is created. It is to exist throughout all eternity. It may become eternal in its attributes by the constant fidelity of a husband and wife to one another and by their faithfulness to their covenants with their Heavenly Father."[96] In the Lord's plan, the sacred bonds of marriage are the holy space—the sanctuary—where the token of the covenant is properly shared between a husband and wife who are faithful to each other and their covenants. This is where the blessing of posterity, as the Lord intended, is ultimately realized.

By no coincidence, Genesis 17 marked the first time where Sarah specifically became Abraham's partner in the covenant. The promises of posterity previously given to Abraham were not specific to Sarah. Only in this chapter did the Lord promise Abraham that his seed and the covenant would flow through Sarah (Genesis 17:19). There was no seed of the covenant without her. Genesis 17 is as much about Sarah as it is Abraham. They both received new names, and they both received the promise of posterity. Then the token of circumcision given to Abraham carried through only with Sarah, as Abraham's wife and the embodiment of a celestial marriage.

Celestial marriage goes hand in hand with chastity because the sacredness of the procreative power is to be exercised only within the bonds of marriage. Properly understood, sexual intimacy is anything but trivial or casual. Likewise, Latter-day Saints should be the last people to consider intimacy awkward or gross. To the contrary, it's sacred. And because it's sacred, it must be kept in its sacred place. Remember that every covenant has its sanctuary. Here, the sanctuary where the token of the covenant is shared is within the bonds of marriage.

When he was president of Brigham Young University, Elder Jeffrey R. Holland taught what I consider to be the finest discourse ever offered on the law of chastity and the sacred procreative power shared by a husband and wife. "Human intimacy, that sacred, physical union ordained of God for a married couple, deals with a *symbol* that demands special sanctity. Such an act of love between a man and a woman is—or certainly was ordained to be—a symbol of total union: union of their hearts, their hopes, their lives, their love, their family, their future, their everything."[97]

Elder Holland continued, "Sexual intimacy is not only a symbolic union between a man and a woman—the uniting of their very souls—but it is also symbolic of a union between mortals and deity, between otherwise ordinary and fallible humans uniting for a rare and special moment with God Himself and all the powers by which He gives life in this wide universe of ours. In this latter sense, human intimacy is a sacrament, a very special kind of symbol."[98] Indeed, the blessings and the purpose of the Abrahamic covenant—eternal posterity and all that the Father hath—are expressed in this act ordained of God for bringing mortal life to God's greatest creation: His children.

On this subject, Elder Holland concluded, "I submit . . . that [we] will never be more like God at any other time in this life than [we] are expressing that particular power."[99]

Understanding the law of chastity and the sacredness of the procreative power, any awkwardness associated with circumcision should be replaced with reverence for the covenant that it signifies and the divine act—the sacrament, as Elder Holland taught—between a husband and wife. That act, when properly understood and reverenced, is the most Godlike act in mortality.

The principle of eternal marriage and its inseparable counterpart, the law of chastity, are preparation for the fulness of the blessings of the Abrahamic covenant: posterity, priesthood, and the celestial kingdom.

- *The Lord commanded Abraham and all the males in his family and stewardship to be circumcised.*
- *The Lord referred to circumcision as the token of the covenant. A token is the physical evidence of a covenant agreement.*
- *According to the* Encyclopedia of Mormonism, *the word* token *denotes "throwing together" of two parts, such as a bone or a piece of wood, to fit together like a lock and key.*

- *This token was an obvious reference to the blessing of posterity, as part of the Abrahamic covenant. Circumcision therefore taught the principle of covenant marriage and the law of chastity.*
- *Elder Jeffrey R. Holland said that the act of physical intimacy between a husband and wife is a symbol of a divine union and is a sacrament in which a husband and wife share in the divine blessing of creation with Heavenly Father.*
- *The teachings of Genesis 17 may therefore be considered preparation for the fulness of the Abrahamic covenant blessings.*

# Genesis 22

## When the Lord Has Thoroughly Proved Him

**Genesis 22 is** the final pronouncement of the complete blessings of the Abrahamic covenant. This final promise was different from the others because of the oath that the Lord swore, removing all conditions and advancing Abraham's Judgment Day (Genesis 22:16). As with all the other works of Abraham, this promise was preceded by a law.

In Genesis 22, the Lord asked obedience, but this obedience required much more faith than the relatively simple commandment to get up and move of Genesis 12.

The Lord asked for a sacrifice on Mount Moriah, as He did in Genesis 15. But this sacrifice was no heifer, goat, or ram. No, the sacrifice that the Lord asked of Abraham was his only begotten son (Hebrews 11:17), in similitude of the sacrifice of the Only Begotten Son of God, slain for the sins of the world.

In Genesis 17, the Lord asked Abraham to live before Him. Here, the Lord was also asking a life to be given. The same promise of posterity given to Abraham and Sarah now seemed lost—when in the Lord's knowledge and plan, it was actually about to multiply.

The laws exemplified by the works of Abraham all build on each other. They are inseparably intertwined. All of them may be considered celestial laws because all of them must be obeyed to receive a celestial glory. Still, this last law required a greater level of obedience, sacrifice, and holiness than the laws given before. A wise man once said, "The Lord does not ask much of us; He asks everything."[100] Abraham was about to learn not just that lesson but also the blessing that comes from such an offering.

## A Lesson on Being like God

In a real sense, the commandment to sacrifice Isaac served to teach Abraham a lesson on godliness. God the Father gave His Only Begotten Son (John 3:16). Now, Abraham was commanded to give his only begotten son as well. In both instances, the sacrifice led to eternal life. When Jesus died on Calvary, the way for eternal life for all of God's children was paved. When Abraham was willing to sacrifice Isaac on Mount Moriah, his eternal life was assured.

## The Sacrifice of All Things

No, we will probably not be asked to sacrifice our children to fulfill this work of Abraham and receive the same blessing. Don't get hung up on the thought of the Lord asking Abraham to kill his own son. Like many Old Testament examples, the lesson we are to learn is found in the symbolism. The real message here is the sacrifice of all things. Of all the sacrifices the Lord could have asked of Abraham, Isaac had to be the most difficult. President Harold B. Lee said, "The most important of all the commandments of God is that one that you're having the most difficulty keeping today. If it's one of dishonesty, if it's one of unchastity, if it's one of falsifying, not telling the truth, today is the day for you to work on that until you've been able to conquer that weakness. Then you start on the next one that's most difficult for you to keep."[101]

In Abraham's case, the most difficult commandment to keep—the most costly sacrifice he could offer—was that of his son. But the blessing just for being willing to offer this sacrifice was eternal life.

Joseph Smith's teaching on the price of eternal life illustrates the principle perfectly.

> Let us here observe, that a religion that does not require the sacrifice of all things never has power sufficient to produce the faith necessary unto life and salvation; for, from the first existence of man, the faith necessary unto the enjoyment of life and salvation never could be obtained without the sacrifice of all earthly things. It was through this sacrifice, and this only, that God has ordained that men should enjoy eternal life; and it is through the medium of the sacrifice of all earthly things that men do actually know that they are doing the things that are well pleasing in the sight of God. When a man has offered in sacrifice all that he has for the truth's sake, not even withholding his life, and believing before God that he has been called to make this sacrifice because he seeks to do his will, he does know, most assuredly, that God does and will accept his sacrifice and offering, and that he has not, nor will not seek his face in vain. Under these circumstances, then, he can obtain the faith necessary for him to lay hold on eternal life.[102]

The Savior taught the same concept in His parable of the pearl of great price. "Again, the kingdom of heaven is like unto a merchant man, seeking goodly pearls: who, when he had found one pearl of great price, went and sold all that he had, and bought it" (Matthew 13:45–46). The celestial inheritance is worth going and selling all that we have. The sacrifice of all things pays eternal dividends in this covenant.

In Genesis 22, Abraham was promised eternal life after the ultimate trial of his faith, the ultimate test of his obedience, the ultimate act of walking before God. Abraham was willing to give everything, so the Lord was willing to give Abraham His every blessing, even all that the He hath. This is consecration. Abraham's willingness to sacrifice all things, even his own son, was consecration incarnate.

## The Abrahamic Covenant, the Temple, and the Atonement

The geography of Genesis 22 is in some ways as poignant as the *akedah* ("binding") itself. The Lord commanded Abraham specifically to take Isaac to Mount Moriah to offer him as a sacrifice (Genesis 22:2). This is the same place where the temple of Solomon was later built (2 Chronicles 3:1). This is no coincidence. This is a clear and marvelous lesson on the Abrahamic covenant and the sanctuary of the covenant—the temple. Mount Moriah was not just where the blessings of the covenant were promised; it was where the blessings were unconditionally sealed.

The altar on Mount Moriah was the most sacred of all sanctuaries of the covenant. Here, Abraham not only offered the greatest sacrifice he could offer, but he received the greatest promise he could receive: the promise of eternal life, eternal families, eternal priesthood, and eternal inheritance.

And the connection does not stop there. Mount Moriah was also the site of the sacrifice of the Only Begotten Son. Golgotha is actually a part of this same holy mountain. The Atonement is the foundation of every temple ordinance. It was only fitting that the temple would be built not just on the spot where the sacrifice of the Savior was so perfectly prefigured, but also where the great and last sacrifice actually was wrought.

On Mount Moriah, the Abrahamic covenant, the temple, and the Atonement all reached their zenith. The three are inseparably and beautifully connected. The temple exists to bestow the blessings of the Abrahamic covenant, and those blessings represent the full power, majesty, and beauty of the Atonement. They *are* the Atonement, made alive in the lives of those who receive and honor every covenant and ordinance of the temple.

## The Holy Spirit of Promise

You have no doubt noticed how each of the laws given to Abraham—each of the works of Abraham that we are to follow—parallels the first principles and ordinances of the gospel. In accepting Abraham's consecration and bestowing the irrevocable gift of eternal life, the final ordinance in the fourth article of faith was likewise paralleled. The laying on of hands for the gift of the Holy Ghost was prefigured in Abraham's willingness to sacrifice all things because it was there that the Holy Spirit of promise was manifest. "If a man marry a wife by my word, which is my law, and by the new and everlasting covenant, and it is sealed unto them by the Holy Spirit of promise . . . it shall be said unto them—Ye shall come forth in the first resurrection; . . . and shall inherit thrones, kingdoms, principalities, and powers, dominions, all heights and depths" (D&C 132:19).

The ultimate test that leads to the ultimate blessing—the fulness of the Abrahamic covenant and the priesthood—is the sacrifice of all things. This means complete and absolute obedience and sacrifice. It means complete walking before God to the point of perfection. It means absolute fidelity and devotion not just to God but also to one's eternal spouse, who is the essential third party to the highest of covenants. It means freshly cleaned feet from having walked before God in all these commandments.

At that point, the Lord's promise is to all of us, just as it was to Abraham—eternal posterity, eternal priesthood, and an eternal inheritance in the celestial kingdom.

- *Genesis 22 marks the final promise of the complete blessings of the Abrahamic covenant.*
- *Building on the laws of sacrifice, obedience, and walking before God, the Lord asked Abraham to offer the single most difficult sacrifice he could possibly offer: his only begotten son.*
- *Not only was this a lesson to Abraham on how to be like God the Father, it was also a commandment of consecration and the sacrifice of all things.*
- *The Lord commanded Abraham to travel to Mount Moriah to sacrifice Isaac. Mount Moriah was the place where the temple of Solomon was built. Golgotha was likewise a part of Mount Moriah.*
- *Therefore, in Mount Moriah, we see the unmistakable connection between the Abrahamic covenant, the temple, and the Atonement.*
- *The commandment to sacrifice all things (in this case, Isaac) also typifies a parallel to the first principles and ordinances of the gospel, in that it symbolizes the Holy Spirit of Promise sealing the covenant of exaltation.*

# Endnotes

1. John A. Widtsoe, "Temple Worship," *Best Loved Talks of the LDS People* (Salt Lake City: Deseret Book, 2002), 475.
2. Hugh Nibley, *Abraham and Egypt* (Salt Lake City: Deseret Book, 1981), 653.
3. Robert L. Millett, *LDS Beliefs—A Doctrinal Reference* (Salt Lake City: Deseret Book, 2011), 18; see also Doctrine and Covenants 27:10; 98:32.
4. Joseph Fielding Smith, *Teachings of the Prophet Joseph Smith* (Salt Lake City: Deseret Book, 1976), 91.
5. Joseph Fielding Smith, *Doctrines of Salvation* (Salt Lake City: Bookcraft, 1954–56), 2:241.
6. Boyd K. Packer, "Charge to the David O. McKay School of Education," December 1996.
7. John A. Widtsoe, "Temple Worship," *Best Loved Talks of the LDS People*, 486.
8. Ezra Taft Benson, "What I Hope You Will Teach Your Children about the Temple," *Ensign*, August 1985.

9. Broadly speaking, there are two main differences between the accounts in Genesis 12 and Abraham 2. First, Genesis 12 does not mention the priesthood as one of the blessings and the means of blessing promised to Abraham in Abraham 2. Second, Genesis 12 does not mention Abraham's seed and the blessings they would be to the world. In the plain text of Abraham 2, both of these differences are references to the priesthood.
10. This section in particular lends itself to rereading. These biblical scholars likely had no idea how much of the restored gospel system of covenants they have described. Their observations came purely from the Bible with no reference to the teachings of the restored gospel of Jesus Christ or the restored temple.
11. Kevin Conner and Ken Malmin, *The Covenants* (Portland: City Bible Publishing, 1983), 5–7.
12. Ibid.
13. Ronald H. Taurel, *Marriage: The Forgotten Covenant* (Maitland, Florida: Xulon Press, 2008), 45.
14. John A. Widtsoe, *Discourses of Brigham Young* (Salt Lake City: Deseret Book, 1954), 416.
15. Most of the references to the priesthood in the scriptures are not capitalized, except when the reference is specific to the Melchizedek Priesthood or the Aaronic Priesthood. This reference in section two is capitalized, as are the references in Abraham 2:9 and 11, where the Abrahamic covenant is first introduced.
16. See Joseph Fielding McConkie and Robert L. Millet, *Joseph Smith: The Choice Seer* (Salt Lake City: Deseret Book, 1986), 187.
17. Theodore M. Burton, "The Power of Elijah," *Ensign*, May 1974; emphasis added.
18. Joseph Fielding Smith, *Teachings of the Prophet Joseph Smith*, 322; emphasis added.

19. Ibid., 323.
20. Ibid.
21. "What Every Elder Should Know—and Every Sister as Well: A Primer on Principles of Priesthood Government," *Ensign*, February 1993.
22. Ezra Taft Benson, "What I Hope You Will Teach Your Children about the Temple."
23. Joseph Fielding Smith, *Teachings of the Prophet Joseph Smith*, 308.
24. Leland B. Nelson, *The Journal of Joseph* (Provo: Council Press, 1979), 190.
25. Ibid., 191; emphasis added.
26. John A. Widtsoe, *Discourses of Brigham Young*, 416.
27. Joseph Fielding Smith, "The Pearl of Great Price," *Best Loved Talks of the LDS People*, 459.
28. Ibid.
29. Joseph Fielding Smith, *Teachings of the Prophet Joseph Smith*, 159.
30. Ezra Taft Benson, "What I Hope You Will Teach Your Children about the Temple."
31. Dallin H. Oaks, "The Keys and Authority of the Priesthood," *Ensign*, May 2014.
32. M. Russell Ballard, "Men and Women in the Work of the Lord," *New Era*, April 2014.
33. Archibald Bennett, *Saviors on Mount Zion* (Salt Lake City: Deseret Sunday School Union, 1958), 194.
34. Joseph Fielding Smith, *Teachings of the Prophet Joseph Smith*, 38–39.
35. Thank you, Noel Reynolds, for this insight.
36. Archibald Bennett, *Saviors on Mount Zion*, 194.
37. Howard W. Hunter, *Wisdom of the Prophets—Temple Worship* (Sandy, Utah: Leatherwood Press, 2006).

38. Archibald Bennett, *Saviors on Mount Zion*, 194.
39. E. Douglas Clark, *The Blessings of Abraham—Becoming a Zion People* (American Fork, Utah: Covenant Communications, 2005), 179.
40. Hugh Nibley, *Temple and Cosmos* (Salt Lake City: Deseret Book, 1992), 52.
41. E. Douglas Clark, *The Blessings of Abraham—Becoming a Zion People*, 179.
42. Ibid., 137.
43. Joseph Fielding Smith, *Teachings of the Prophet Joseph Smith*, 322–23.
44. The pronoun *ye* used here is plural. The Lord was speaking to Joseph Smith, but not to him alone. He was speaking to everyone who is a part of the Abrahamic covenant, as seen in the next verse.
45. Clyde J. Williams, *The Teachings of Harold B. Lee* (Salt Lake City: Bookcraft, 1996), 256.
46. Ibid.
47. R. Clayton Brough and Thomas W. Grassley, *Understanding Patriarchal Blessings* (Springville, Utah: Horizon Publishers, 1984), 89.
48. Harold B. Lee, "From the Valley of Despair to the Mountain Peaks of Hope," *New Era*, August 1971.
49. Rossiter W. Raymond, "Death Is Only a Horizon."
50. E. Douglas Clark, *The Blessings of Abraham—Becoming a Zion People*, 161.
51. Ibid., 197.
52. In the eternal perspective, Abraham's descendants, through all of his children, are still invited to receive these blessings as they repent, accept Jesus Christ, and enter into the same covenant as Isaac.
53. Jennifer Clark Lane, "The Lord Will Redeem His People," *Thy People Shall Be My People and Thy God My God* (Salt Lake City: Deseret Book, 1994), 53.

54. William Smith, *Smith's Bible Dictionary* (Westwood: Barbour and Company, Inc., 1987), 213.
55. Joseph Fielding Smith, *Teachings of the Prophet Joseph Smith*, 157.
56. E. Douglas Clark, *The Blessings of Abraham—Becoming a Zion People*, 166.
57. Joseph Fielding Smith, *Teachings of the Prophet Joseph Smith*, 157.
58. Oscar W. McConkie Jr., *Angels* (Salt Lake City: Deseret Book, 1975), 62.
59. Jennifer Clark Lane, "The Lord Will Redeem His People," *Thy People Shall Be My People and Thy God My God*, 58–59.
60. Joseph Fielding Smith, "The Pearl of Great Price," *Best Loved Talks of the LDS People*, 462.
61. "The Family: A Proclamation to the World," *Ensign*, November 1995.
62. Sheri Dew, "Are We Not All Mothers?" *Ensign*, November 2001.
63. Ibid.
64. Joseph Fielding Smith, *Teachings of the Prophet Joseph Smith*, 297.
65. Kevin Conner and Ken Malmin, *The Covenants*, 5.
66. Joseph Fielding Smith, *Teachings of the Prophet Joseph Smith*, 298–99.
67. Ibid.
68. Ibid., 366.
69. Ezra Taft Benson, "What I Hope You Will Teach Your Children about the Temple."
70. Joseph Fielding Smith, *Teachings of the Prophet Joseph Smith*, 150.
71. E. Douglas Clark, *The Blessings of Abraham—Becoming a Zion People*, 82.

72. Marion G. Romney, "Temples—The Gates to Heaven," *Ensign*, March 1971.
73. Joseph Fielding Smith, *Teachings of the Prophet Joseph Smith*, 304–5.
74. The Bible is rife with references to Israel bearing the Abrahamic covenant. See Deuteronomy 7:8; 29:9–13; 1 Chronicles 16:16; Psalm 105:8–10; Jeremiah 11:5; Micah 7:20; Luke 1:72–73; and Acts 7:17.
75. Hugh Nibley, *Abraham in Egypt*, 334.
76. Orson F. Whitney, in Conference Report, April 1929, 10.
77. James E. Faust, "Dear Are the Sheep That Have Wandered," *Ensign*, May 2003, 62.
78. Stephen L. Richards, *Wisdom of the Prophets—Temple Worship*.
79. Ibid.
80. See Matthew 4:19; 8:19, 22; 9:9; 10:38; 16:24; 19:21, 27; Mark 1:18; 2:14; 8:34; 10:21, 28; Luke 5:11, 27; 9:23, 57, 59–61; John 1:40, 43; 8:12; 10:27; 12:26; and 21:22.
81. S. Dilworth Young, "Obedience—The First Law of Heaven," in Conference Report, April 1966.
82. Joseph Smith, *History of The Church of Jesus Christ of Latter-day Saints*, edited by B. H. Roberts, 7 vols. (Salt Lake City: The Church of Jesus Christ of Latter-day Saints, 1932–51), 2:170.
83. "Commencement Address," in *Commencement Exercises*, Brigham Young University Speeches of the Year (May 31, 1957), 4–5.
84. E. Douglas Clark, *The Blessings of Abraham—Becoming a Zion People*, 147.
85. Joseph Fielding Smith, *Teachings of the Prophet Joseph Smith*, 305.
86. E. Douglas Clark, *The Blessings of Abraham—Becoming a Zion People*, 147.
87. Ibid., 148.
88. As quoted by E. Douglas Clark, *The Blessings of Abraham—Becoming a Zion People*, 164.

89. Bruce R. McConkie, in Conference Report, October 1968.
90. William R. Bradford, "The Safety of the Gospel Law," *Ensign*, November 1977.
91. Donna B. Nielsen, *Beloved Bridegroom* (Salt Lake City: Onyx Press, 1999), 99.
92. John A. Widtsoe, *Discourses of Brigham Young*, 416; emphasis added.
93. Vaugn J. Featherstone, "A Self-Inflicted Purging," *Ensign*, May 1975.
94. Todd Compton, "Symbolism," *The Encyclopedia of Mormonism*, 1428.
95. Joseph Fielding Smith, *Teachings of the Prophet Joseph Smith*, 159.
96. David B. Haight, *Wisdom of the Prophets—Temple Worship.*
97. Jeffrey R. Holland, *Of Souls, Symbols, and Sacraments* (Salt Lake City: Deseret Book, 2001), 17.
98. Ibid., 27.
99. Ibid., 31.
100. As stated by Lennis Knighton, a former mission president whose son, David, was my last companion on my mission in Portugal.
101. Harold B. Lee, *Church News*, May 5, 1973, 3.
102. Joseph Smith, *Lectures on Faith* (Salt Lake City: Deseret Book, 1985), 6:7.

# About the Author

**Mark Shields has** been happily married to his wife, Cami, since 1992. They are the proud parents of five daughters—Heidi, Kayla, Claire, Anna, and Robyn— and one son-in-law, Jamison. He practices as an attorney in Mesa, Arizona, where the family has lived since 2001. He has competed in a number of races, including the 2015 Boston Marathon, and enjoys building high-quality speakers and other stereo equipment in his spare time. He's served in many capacities, including bishop; temple and missionary preparation instructor; Primary, nursery, seminary, and Sunday School teacher; high councilor; and temple worker.

He is grateful to Doug Holt, Cory Jensen, Stephanie Underwood, and Traci Larson for their wonderful help in editing and revising this book.

Mark is pleased to add *Your Covenant* to his other works, which include *Your Endowment*, *Gospel Symbols,* and *Holy Gifts*.

**SCAN** to visit

WWW.MARKSHIELDSAUTHOR.COM